Buddha and the Dancing Girl is so warmly and gently written, her lessons learned quickly become our own. Reading about the author's life varied explorations of diverse dimensions of possible experience help us to energize, validate, and increase attention to our own spiritual consciousness.

Arthur Kornhaber, M.D., American Board of Psychiatry and Neurology, *Spirit*

Buddha and the Dancing Girl is a story of inner and outer adventures, from acting in New York to writing in Hollywood, and from a girlhood in Texas to a spiritual search in India — a life fully lived, offering us remarkable experiences, memorable people, and deep wisdom. What a privilege to read about this life!

Betty Sue Flowers, Ph.D., editor, *Joseph Campbell and The Power of Myth*

You inspired me through your new book, *Buddha and the Dancing Girl.* I can't quite explain how I was inspired but it has something to do with the way you described the opposites in your life coming together, and the way events can define and alter our lives.

Dixie Gladstone

Every page offers stories, insights, or wisdom that we can "take home." Meanwhile, we eagerly turn the pages, wondering what will happen next. In *Buddha and the Dancing Girl*, Catherine Ann Jones generously shares experiences most of us will never have: acting on the stage and screen, living for years in a South

Indian hut, writing award-winning plays and screenplays, and lecturing internationally. Yet her memoir offers a deeper gift: spiritual and psychological wisdom distilled from a lifetime of reflection. Most memoirs inform us about the author. In *Buddha and the Dancing Girl,* Catherine Ann Jones teaches us about ourselves.

Dianne Skafte, Ph.D., Listening to the Oracle

Catherine's outer life and accomplishments is matched in its richness only by her inner spiritual life. What a life lived! Catherine balances the tug of war of opposites — the inner spiritual world in one hand, the outer world of theater, acting, writing in the other — with the grace and beauty of a ballerina. *Buddha and the Dancing Girl* is a beautiful and fascinating read that I literally could not put down.

Molly Jordan Koch, Co-author of Magic Time: My Life
in Hollywood

Buddha and the Dancing Girl perfectly describes the difference between ordinary time and the Story that emerges in this moving remembrance/creation. I couldn't put it down. Catherine Ann Jones gives us a life with two centers, art and the spiritual quest: one center lies beyond the other and gives it purpose. As her title implies, she dances for the sake of a deeper reality.

Al Collins, Ph.D., Fatherson: A Self Psychology of the
Archetypal Masculine

Books by Catherine Ann Jones

The Way of Story: The Craft & Soul of Writing

Heal Your Self with Writing

What Story Are You Living?

Freud's Oracle

True Fables: Stories from Childhood

Buddha and the Dancing Girl: A Creative Life

East is West (Stories of India)

Buddha

and the

Dancing Girl

A Creative Life

Catherine Ann Jones

Prasana Press

Published by Prasana Press

105 S. Arnaz Ave, Ojai, CA 93023 USA

www.wayofstory.com

catherinejones@wayofstory.com

ISBN 978-0-9765352-4-9 (paperback)

Buddha and the Dancing Girl by Catherine Ann Jones

Copyright @2020 by Catherine Ann Jones

Book Layout by Mayo Morley

1. Memoir
2. Theatre and Film
3. Spirituality

For the Householder Sage

Those who take refuge in Me alone
Shall cross over this maya (illusion).

The Bhagavad Gita

Table of Contents

Prologue

Part I: Creative Beginnings: New Orleans, Japan, Texas

Part II: Marriage, Motherhood, & Separation: France, Ireland, New York

Part III: Awakening: India

Part IV: Lure of the Greasepaint: New York

Part V: Touched by Angels: Hollywood

Part VI: Harbor & Home: Ojai, California

Epilogue

Prologue

The Continuous Thread of Revelation

Events in our lives happen in a sequence of time,
but in their significance to ourselves,
they find their own order...
the continuous thread of revelation.

Eudora Welty

I can remember myself at age seven, sitting outside and watching the long stretch of a grassy Texas lawn and an endless driveway dotted with rose bushes, waiting ... waiting for someone to come and carry me away to my rightful place. Even as a small child, I knew I did not belong here, that this place was not home. Strange how even when very young, we know where we belong and where we don't. These people were not my people. I was right, though it would be many years before I would find my tribe.

The specifics of seekers' and creative lives vary in details but they all usually share one thing in common. There is often from an early age a longing for the spiritual or religious life and/or for a life of meaning and purpose, which may take twists and turns before discovering their own path and giving expression to what they've found. Such individuals forego a historical or literal style of living and are drawn instead to a timeless creative life.

My journey would take me to south India searching for Truth, to New York and the world of the theatre, to Hollywood writing for the stars and later travelling the world offering writing workshops. Expressed through the writing of plays, movies, and books, all these chapters have merged into a healing journey from childhood abuse to love and a challenging marriage, motherhood, creative fulfillment and success, memorable relationships, and the slow, sure evolution of the soul.

All journeys are a journey back to Self. I have always felt — and keenly so — that there exists something greater than one's smaller self and that it is a privilege to be called to surrender and to serve this Force in whatever way possible.

Perhaps sharing one seeker's journey and insights gained along the way may echo and give meaning to your own. At least, that is the intention for this book.

Catherine Ann Jones
Ojai, CA, 2020

PART 1   Creative Beginnings
New Orleans, Japan, Texas

Life can only be understood backwards, but it must be lived forwards.

Soren Kierkegaard

Dorothy and Capt. Dack Jones with Catherine, age 2

Immediately following WW II, my mother and I left New Orleans to join 'Captain Jones', as my father was called, in Japan where he was stationed post war. My father said that we would live in Tokyo and Sendai for the next two years. It was all a bit of a puzzle when you're too little to understand everything.

My mother and I travelled on a great ship for many days, sailing from America to Japan. It was a grand adventure. Once I got lost and thought the laundry chute was a slide to play on, so I climbed up and enjoyed going down the slide then falling into a pile of white sheets. I was told never to do that again, and I didn't. But it was fun! Soon after we arrived in Tokyo, I fell sick and had to be taken to a hospital. There they operated and removed my tonsils so I couldn't talk for a while. What I remember is being given ice cream after the operation — very tasty.

We lived in a nice, airy house full of light, with five Japanese servants. Meneko was my nanny and I liked her a lot. From her, I quickly learned to speak Japanese and would translate between the servants and my parents. Children learn other languages much easier than grown-ups or so I was later told. (Years later, my son and I lived in south India when he was two to four years old — the same time span as myself in Japan — and he quickly learned Malayalam, the language of Kerala in south India. But that's another story.)

My father had a pet monkey who was very jealous of anyone who came near. The monkey would screech loudly and try to bite me when I wanted to sit on my father's lap. Mean little monkey. I forget his name, probably because I didn't like him.

One Sunday afternoon, we went outside Tokyo to a tremendous park in a place called Kamakura. Cherry trees were in bloom and they smelled like honey. We saw bright pink flowers on the trees everywhere. We sat down and had a picnic. My mother told me years later that when I saw little children who looked hungry, I would give away our food to them. Meneko, my nanny, wanted to show me something special and took me away. After lunch, we walked to a nearby temple.

It was there in Kamakura that I first saw God — the enormous Kamakura Buddha, thirty-five feet tall. At first, I thought it was a mountain. It was so big, giant. Yet when we got close, I gazed up and there He was. I remember feeling very small as I raised my eyes up at this beautiful man who was very, very big. His eyes were closed and his face seemed to be smiling. Meneko told me softly that this was Lord Buddha. I couldn't talk for some time but remember looking up at Him and thinking, "Oh, this is what they mean by God." It was very peaceful there, and though I was only four, I never forgot Him. Ever since that day, I always felt that there was something far greater than human beings. I also felt protected by this something far greater than I was. This feeling stayed with me though the image of what God is would change as I grew up.

Kamakura Buddha in Japan

Much later I understood that God wasn't a bronze statue or a painting of some religious deity or god, but was that deep, deep feeling inside that there is something far greater than man, and it is always there watching over us. Once you know this, it doesn't really matter what God looks like. The deity may look different to different people, to people all over this world. It's more than enough to know this Presence is ever there, and that it never, never goes away.

Seeing the colossal statue of the Kamakura Buddha was

one of the two most powerful memories from my years in Japan. That same year, at age four, another experience captured my soul. I was excited to see for the first time colorful, Japanese dancers on stage at a cherry blossom festival in the park outside Tokyo. I felt that I belonged on stage with these dancing girls. I ran away because I wanted to join the company and be 'a dancing girl.' Two hours later I was found. My parents were relieved and I promised never to run away again. Yet the desire to act and dance would remain.

Somehow these two imprints at an early age would forecast the direction my life would later take. These two events mirrored a tension I would experience all of my life, a tension of opposites. They marked the beginning of a religious or spiritual quest intertwined with a love of self-expression through drama. C. G. Jung writes of this tension of opposites: "If the individual succeeds in giving collective validity to his widened consciousness, he creates a tension of opposites that provides the stimulation which culture needs for its further progress." Here lies an excellent definition of the artist. It seems also that this tension of opposites propels us into what the Greeks might call our destiny or fate. These two opposing poles would remain for me a spiritual quest for meaning combined with a path of creative expression or purpose as actor, playwright, screenwriter, and author of books. All too often, the tension of opposite tendencies created a tug of war within, yet, happily, once in a while they would merge into some creative form such as a play, film, or book — all with spiritual overtones.

Catherine, age 6

The roots of my beginnings were planted long before I was born. It is my experience that we are more or less born knowing who we are. The soul carries imprints from ancestors as well as from past lives and these become *vasanas* or tendencies from long before we are born. These tendencies serve to guide us in the next life. We can choose to either follow that guidance or resist it — that is, resist being who we were born to be. Insights often arise early on as signposts indicating the direction each individual life will take. The two imprints from Japan when I was only four years old would remain within as a magnet drawing me to what some call destiny.

From my Celtic ancestors came a legacy of resilience, boundless courage, and fierce determination. I witnessed these same traits in my maternal grandmother. The memory of her quiet strength, genuine undemonstrative goodness, and unassuming power inspire me still. Our people left Scotland and Ireland in 1646 and settled in Virginia. In 1862 during the Civil War in America, the men folk were off fighting for the South. After the Yankees had burned down the barn, the women and children joined a wagon train and fled from Virginia to Texas. My ancestor, Mrs. Haggard, writes in her diaries, "We had been in distress but not discouraged. We knew no such word as fail." Against the greatest of odds, these women and children reached their destination, the Dallas area in Texas, where their descendants live to this day. Their spirit lives on and has come to my aid many times in New York, Hollywood, England, France, India, Greece, Kuwait, and other far-flung places where I have lived, worked, and now teach writing workshops.

On my maternal grandfather's side, books on our family history say we are descended from those who later came to be known as the royal Windsors of England. To keep this lineage alive, the eldest son of each generation was to be named 'Windsor' so I had an Uncle Windsor, my grandfather's elder brother and business partner. However, I was more impressed that through my maternal grandmother's side lies a direct, ancestral line to 19th century pioneer rifleman hero and Congressman Davy Crockett whose passion for freedom ended in his death in the defense of the Alamo in San Antonio, Texas. The tendency to project ideals unto causes or quests persists in me to this day.

There are other tendencies inherited from the past from my Calvinistic, Puritan background: delayed gratification, one-pointed focus on work or duty, exaggerated independence, and self-denial. Being aware of these traits has helped me to temper them while at the same time honor those same traits that enabled past generations to survive and prosper.

My maternal grandmother who grew up on a farm in north Texas, a college graduate and a teacher of Latin, was also a solid example of those early pioneer women. One rainy afternoon, she was talking about her past with me, describing how her neighbors shared their crops with one another during the Depression, a challenging time in 1930s America. "Oh," I said, "you mean you bartered." "No," she replied firmly. "We gave. We gave, and they gave." With this simple correction, she enabled me to see the past with her eyes. Her perspective was quite different from that of my own generation, for her perspective had more heart. This casual exchange remains a valued legacy long after this wonderful woman is gone. I remember, too, how when I was sick as a child, my grandmother would put me in her bed during the day rather than in my upstairs room. She would place a small silver bell next to the bed so whenever I needed anything, I would just ring and she would come. Gram, a constant, loving presence.

Even now, I sometimes imagine my 'Gram', her clear blue eyes full of life, goodness, and understanding, standing behind me. (Over the years, at least two psychics I have seen have commented — unasked — on seeing her standing behind me, describing her to a T!)

Memories are carried not only in our conscious and unconscious memory, but also in our senses. For instance, even now, if I smell an apple pie baking anywhere, my grandmother is instantly present. Positive memories can serve as a powerful ally, for heart memory is stronger even than death.

After two memorable years in Japan, the family returned to New Orleans where I had been born. I was four and sensitive to the increasing discord between my parents. In Japan, my mother had never felt at ease in a country that until recently had been declared an enemy and threat. My father was personally decorated by President Eisenhower for outstanding courage in the Pacific during the war, yet unfortunately for all of us, the imprints and the trauma of war lived on in him. Years later, as other soldiers who suffered from what would be labeled post-traumatic stress, my father could not settle easily into post-war domesticity.

Anyone who has survived childhood has enough material to last a lifetime.

Flannery O'Connor

In my writing classes and workshops, I tell my students that if you want to be a writer and you come from happy families, I am sorry for you. There is no better background for a writer than a dysfunctional family. The response is always laughter and yet there is some truth in this as early discord often provides the stuff of which drama and art are made. Sometimes a missing piece of childhood often propels the artist to create another world entirely, a world better than the one he or she was born into. It may also serve to create a spiritual longing for something more, something greater than our small selves.

Soon after our return to New Orleans, my volatile father took the savings my mother had worked for during the war years and ran away. Avoiding a divorce summons, he returned and without notice, carried me away to Mississippi to stay with his sister whom I had never met. He told me I'd never see my mother again. Then that same evening, after he read to me a Golden Book story about a devoted father taking his young daughter to the circus and buying for her a red balloon, disappeared as I slept — without saying good-bye. He was alerted that the police were after him for kidnapping me so he fled. As a child of four, I believed then that I would never see either of my parents again, and experienced a deep-rooted realization of being solely on my own. We learned later that my father had re-enlisted in the Army, becoming years later a Ltd. Colonel. Every three or four years he would re-appear for a day, remaining a remote mythic figure in my life.

Two days after I had been kidnapped and carried away to the red clay hills of Mississippi, the police came and carried me home to New Orleans and to my grandparents and mother. Yet to this day, whenever I see red clay anywhere in the world, I am once again that four-year-old child held hostage in a small white framed house with strangers in the red hills of Mississippi. And I am alone.

Receive as many blows as possible in this life,
Only then will the heart turn upward.

Sri Ramakrishna

Like my father before me, I had both petit-mal and grand-mal epilepsy when young starting at a year and a half. At age four, one seizure was so violent that my mother drove me to a hospital in New Orleans. The oxygen tank was not working.

Somehow, I stopped breathing, turned blue, and was officially declared dead. My mother became hysterical and ran outside, screaming, "My daughter is dead! My daughter is dead!" After a moment, as a last resort, the doctor gave mouth to mouth resuscitation and brought me back to life. Years later I read that sometimes this can mean that the soul you were born with has finished its work and departs while a new soul enters the body. I don't know if that's true or not, but find it both interesting as well as probable.

A divorced mother in the 1950s — especially in the south — was considered an outcast. All my friends had both a mother and father living with them. My mother was always concerned with status and never recovered from the social stigma of having had a failed marriage. Her bitterness was often turned towards me, and once she angrily told me that my father left us because of me. He didn't want to be burdened with a child. Of course, I accepted this as true — as children do. It was all my fault. A sensual woman living with her parents and not dating, she was, for many years, deeply frustrated and would sometimes beat me passionately. Her weapon of choice was a braided leather belt which left colorful, red welts. Sometimes she would use a clothes hanger or her strong nails that were lethal, leaving to this day, one white scar on my upper left arm above the elbow. The odd thing was that instead of breaking my spirit, she created of me a committed rebel and independent spirit. It was as if her brutal cruelty provided something hard to push against, enabling me, in time, to become strong.

Years later, I felt compassion, seeing her as a woman who was bright and might have been a lawyer or a businesswoman instead of a secretary. Had she been born in my generation, perhaps she would have done more with her innate gifts. All too often, women of her generation opted for underpaid jobs rather than careers. Necessity pressured them to do so. Consequently, she always felt a kind of unexpressed envy for me and yet at the same time, a parent's pride, as I went to New York then Hollywood to pursue and succeed in a chosen career. However, the pride she felt was never expressed directly to me, only to friends and other family members as she would share news of my successes and awards with them.

The blessing was that my mother and I lived with her parents. My grandmother mothered and even spoiled me. Thanks to Gram, I learned what unconditional love was, a lesson one never forgets. I am not sure that anyone can learn to love if they have never themselves been loved. Thankfully, I was.

I've learned that people will forget what you said, people will forget what you did, but people will never forget how you made them feel.

Maya Angelou

15

From New Orleans to Texas

When I was seven, the family (Gram and Daddy Milt, Mary, my mother's youngest sister, Mother, and I) returned to Texas, this time to Irving, a satellite suburb near downtown Dallas. In New Orleans before we moved, Daddy Milt and his elder brother, Windsor, had built a successful bakery business which went national: Hubig's Pies, best known for Hubig's Pocket Fruit Pies. My gentle grandfather, having worked sixteen hours a day in the pie business, was diagnosed with Parkinson's Disease, and retired at age forty.

My maternal family had been settled in Texas since 1862 when they fled Virginia during the American Civil War and wagon-trained to the Dallas area. So, when my grandfather retired early from Hubig's pies in New Orleans, it seemed natural to return to Texas. They purchased a lovely, large two-story home on a five-acre parcel near Dallas. There was a long driveway leading up to our great white house across from which was a large rose garden. In the center of the garden stood a standing bird bath. Next to the rose garden, under the shade of ancient oak trees, was an outdoor picnic area. The sprawling front grassy yard was the size of a football field and many impromptu games were held there with the neighborhood children — mostly boys. I was especially good at kicking the football barefoot to great distances. To this day, I do not like to wear shoes, and discard them at any opportunity.

Being a Texas tomboy, I loved being in the country even though we were actually living in what was then a small town, Irving, ten minutes from downtown Dallas. My grandparents planted corn and vegetables and also raised chickens, selling eggs to local stores. Both my grandparents had been born on a Texas farm a few miles from each other and it seemed comforting to them to return to their roots. I did not, however, gain a great respect for the fifteen hundred chickens, having to clean out their pens, clip their wings, and perform various other unpleasant duties. I learned that chickens are not terribly bright and could be quite savage, turning on their own kind — hence the term 'pecking order'. Nonetheless, as an only child, I adored animals and was constantly rescuing other birds and small mammals. Late at night and early morning, I might be feeding a mockingbird or dove or a deserted baby rabbit with an eye dropper. The momentous event would be freeing them once they were restored to health. It was a wonderful feeling to release a turtledove into the air or toss a healed bunny onto the grass and watch them soar or hop away. I hold freedom high and try to avoid possessiveness with all living beings — even the two-legged variety.

Every Easter, my grandparents would gift me with a new pet — a bunny or parakeet and once fifty colored baby chicks!

My favorite Easter pet was a little black lamb I named Danny. I raised him from bottle feeding to maturity, but unfortunately, he was a bit prickly with others. Danny would run and buck people from behind as they crossed the pasture. One day I came home from elementary school and Danny was gone. And no one would say how that came to be so. Years later I learned that my grandparents had sold him to the butcher. I felt this as a betrayal of huge proportions. I think now though that what upset me most was not being told. Often it is the secret surrounding hurtful acts that cut deepest.

For several years, I would sleepwalk, getting up from my bed in the middle of the night, still sound asleep, and doing a walkabout. My room was on the second floor and one time I was discovered the next morning sleeping outside on the wet grass. I had no idea how I got there. Where was I trying to go? What was I escaping from?

I spent considerable time lying on the grass and gazing at drifting white clouds, imagining all shapes and forms in the clouds and the stories that they would inspire. As an only child, I was simply 'let be' for large chunks of time to read, drift, and dream. I credit my development as a storyteller from these long, leisurely, unscheduled hours of a lazy, Texas childhood.

From ages seven to nine, I would gather neighborhood friends together to put on plays that I would write, costume, direct, perform, and charge twenty-five cents for the audience to see — usually parents of the cast and crew. One day in the second grade, my teacher read the first chapter from Jack London's novel, *The Call of the Wild* to us. I was so taken with the story of the wolf that I couldn't wait until the next day to hear what would happen. I shyly approached the teacher and asked if I might borrow the book if I promised to bring it back the very next day. Somehow, she trusted me to do just that and I had the guilty pleasure of reading it to the very end under bedcovers with a flashlight! My devotion to animals, as with books, are a kind of love affair and one I never overcame.

I loved school and adored those few teachers who took an interest and instilled in me a love of learning. One teacher insisted I go from the second to the fourth grade, hence skipping the third grade altogether. This made me the youngest in my class through high school.

One day when I was in the fourth grade, we were to do a report on our ancestors. It was during the time of the popular Disney television series that starred Fess Parker as *Davy Crockett* so I chose to speak of this hero as my ancestor, Davy Crockett, and was shocked when no one believed I was telling the truth! Incensed, I biked home to my grandmother and asked for proof. She dug around and found the photographs and documents, and the next day, I indignantly displayed them to the non-believers, so the class accepted what was true. What I learned for the first time was that you could speak the truth and sometimes not be believed.

My imagination was rampant (all that cloud gazing!) and one day it got me into big trouble. An only child, I longed for an older brother. I longed so much that at age seven, I simply made one up! His name was David and we went everywhere together and played and talked endlessly. In school, students were asked to fill out forms listing our family members, so naturally I put down David Jones with the 'made-up' particulars, later forgetting all about it. Well, days later, a man came to our home at dinner time, asking why David Jones was not in school. As you might guess, Mother scolded me no end for that one. I could only respond by saying, "Well, he's real to me!" Who is to say that what is imagined is less real than anything else? (I still feel this is true.)

There was very little reading material in our Texas home. The only books I can remember lying around were twelve volumes of *The Book of Knowledge* encyclopedia and the *King James Bible*. I read both cover-to-cover at least once, and the *Bible* twice. There was also the *Wall Street Journal* but I never took to it. I was a TV kid. In New Orleans where I was born, we had the first television on our block and the neighborhood kids would gather round to see *Howdy Doody*. I grew up with television and the characters on weekly series (*Father Knows Best* and *Lassie)* became my extended family. They presented an alternative happy family. The fathers never left and the mothers never hit their children.

From the age of seven, I began to have psychic manifestations. For some time, usually just before I would fall asleep, a tall man dressed in a white gown would stand next to the foot of the bed on my left side. Somehow, I was not afraid and sensed that he was a friend who wished me well and came to protect me. Later that year, I was reading the *Book of Knowledge* encyclopedia and saw illustrations of ancient Egypt. Then I realized that my nighttime friend, dressed as an Egyptian priest, had lived long, long ago. Often, I would see faces of those I knew turning into other faces with other costumes from a past era. Only some years later did I understand that I was seeing their past lives. Psychic manifestations came in other ways as well. I would often know who was calling on the telephone before it rang or before I picked up the phone. I would also know when someone was not telling the truth. I was drawn to visit cemeteries and some thought this strange. I could feel that those departed souls needed comfort. Somehow, I was at home with the dead. Was it perhaps because I had died and come back to life at age four?

Writing as self-expression began for me quite early. Here

21

is my first effort at poetry at age seven.

WISHES

I wish I were a little dog
And had a little tail,
I'd do tricks and chase sticks
Like in a doggie tale.

Or I wish I were a little pig
And could waddle in mud all the while.
Children walk around me with laughter
And smile.

Or I wish I were a little bird
In the sky so high,
And could fly around all day
And sing my merry song so gay.

Or I wish I were a little fairy,
And so many playmates in which to play,
And sing and dance and prance all day.

Though I wish to be all these things,
I still remain a child,
Carefree and merry.

Admittedly, a humble beginning though I continued to

journal from age twelve as well as to write poetry throughout high school and college. In high school, I won the national poetry contest two consecutive years and was twice published. Years later I found those winning poems and with my then teenage son, Christopher, we laughed out loud at how derivative of the Lake poets in England they were, and frankly how bad mine were. It made us wonder what the poems that didn't win were like!

My first story was written at age nine. It was called *The Silver Cup* and was about twin foals born, one sickly which the protagonist, a young girl, secretly raises and trains. Three years later, against all odds, he competes with his sibling and wins the silver cup in the big race. I never submitted it anywhere but remember the infinite pleasure of reading it after my mother typed it out for me. Exciting for a young writer, age nine, to see one's work in print!

By the age of twelve, I had found religion and was duly baptized in the First Baptist Church. Baptism means dunking, something you remember. Unfortunately, I had an adverse reaction to our minister, Brother Kinkaid whose sermon style was reminiscent of Puritan Jonathan Edwards. Kinkaid ranted and raved about hell and damnation from his high, towering pulpit. At age fourteen, I left the church. My grandfather was a deacon and made sure our pastor got a new Cadillac every year and my grandmother was very active in the church as well, doing good works without letting anyone know she was doing them. My sweet grandmother did not speak to me for three weeks after I refused to go back to church, and we lived in the same house!

One day she had Brother Kinkaid come over to talk sense to me. Left alone, the pastor, an ex-athlete over six feet tall with strong shoulders and thick white hair, put his hand on my knee, looked at me intensely and told me that if I didn't come back to the church, I would surely go to hell. I took a deep breath and though only fourteen, said, "Brother Kinkaid, I'd rather go to hell than back to your church. I want a church that speaks of the gentle Jesus who beckons the little children unto him." Eventually, I joined a more liberal church, First Christian Church, and became quite active as youth minister, even giving an annual sermon. I also became chaplain at high school and was called upon to offer prayers at assembly and before football games. (You have to be from Texas to understand how important football is.)

Being a Texas girl and a tomboy, my dream was to have a horse. Since age seven, I had learned to ride on my Uncle Grady's farm a few miles away and collected those small plastic horses that girls collect. I read countless horse stories such as *Black Beauty, Thunderhead, Flicka,* and others. I used to sit on my grandparents' bed post imagining it was a real horse and ride and ride until one afternoon I broke the bed post and was told not to do that anymore.

Mr. Lucky

When I was eleven, I came home one day from school and my grandfather took me outside and introduced me to Babe, a large white mare that was to be mine. I immediately climbed up on her and rode. She bucked and threw me into a cactus patch. My grandfather said if I didn't climb back up then and there, the horse would always remember that. So, I did climb back on and Babe never threw me again. Good lesson for life! (Later, my grandmother helped pick out the cactus needles.)

Later, Babe gave birth to Mr. Lucky, so named as he was born on Friday the 13th of April, which just happened to be my birthday! He was sired by Barracuda, a prize thoroughbred from the King Ranch, the largest ranch in Texas. It was love at first sight. Lucky was a chestnut sorrel with a narrow white streak on his face, and three white socks. As any other proud parent, I stopped at the 7-11 on the way to school that Friday and purchased pink bubble gum cigars to hand out to the kids at school. From age twelve to eighteen, Lucky was my main love. Boys came much later. We played together. One game was hide and seek. I would tell him to stay then run away somewhere and hide behind a bush. Then I whistled and he would always find me. Next, I would wait with closed eyes as he ran away and hid. And I would find him. When he turned two, I broke him myself and no one else could ride him. To tell the truth here, all I had to do was climb on him, bareback. He never even tried to toss me. Once a teenage boy whom I did not know climbed over the fence and tried to ride my horse. Well, Lucky just bucked him off then chased him over the barbed wire fence! That made me smile.

I would hurry home from school, stand at the fence and whistle. Then Lucky, half quarter horse, would come barreling up, stopping on a dime just in front of me. I mostly rode bareback and imagined how Indians must have felt before we invaded their lands. Once a large rattlesnake appeared and angrily shook its rattle, Lucky reared up and as I was riding bareback, I slid off over his tail to the ground. Lucky galloped away at the speed of light, leaving me inches from the outraged rattler. I was too angry to be afraid and stood up calling for Lucky. I felt the snake saw I was angrier than he was, so he slid off pretty quick.

Sometimes my grandfather would let me go to nearby friends who had hundreds of wild acres and I could ride bareback for hours in the wide, open spaces. How to convey that feeling of galloping bareback towards an endless horizon, flat yet infinite, with the warmth of a southern Texas sun beating down and the fierce wind in your hair? That never-ending Texas horizon left me with the profound feeling that anything is possible.

Having completed all my required coursework and skipped a grade making me the youngest in my class, I was persuaded to remain in high school my senior year and just take electives. On a whim, I signed up for drama and to my delight, was cast in all the female leads that year. I remember thinking, "Acting is pretty easy. You just learn the lines and remember the blocking." It would be some years later when I was an actor in New York studying with Lee Strasberg and later with Uta Hagen that I realized how mistaken I was, and how acting becomes more and more complex the longer you do it. Learning the lines is only the beginning.

My senior year I played the leading roles in Noel Coward's *Blithe Spirit* and Karen Andre in a play by Ayn Rand, *The Night of January 16th*. The latter play was memorable as it was a courtroom drama with two endings, depending on the audience members selected to be in the jury. So, if found 'guilty', I would act one ending and, if 'not-guilty', the other ending. It was great fun not knowing, each night rendered a different verdict so I was able to act both endings. One night, my grandmother was chosen to be on the jury, so I kind of knew that I'd get the 'not-guilty' that evening. I did, too.

High School in the late fifties and early sixties in Texas was still an innocent time with little social diversity. The mid-sixties revolution was yet to come. Because it was before desegregation, our African-American maid, Leanna, was not allowed to remain in town after dark. She would be driven across the railroad tracks to Bear Creek before the sun set so as not to be arrested for vagrancy. Sometimes the world is not fair. Later at university, I became active in civil rights and when I came home, I drove our devoted maid crazy. I insisted she sit down with me to eat lunch, then later on that she sit in front when I drove her home to Bear Creek. Of course, in her fifties, she would always refuse. Sometimes, the spirit of civil rights takes time for both sides. Years later, Leanna would become the prototype for a main character in my award-winning play, *The Women of Cedar Creek*.

We were mostly WASP and upper-middle class. Friends or boyfriends were never judged by how rich they were or what their parents did, but chosen only because you liked them. Food was rather boring; it was years before I knew that fish and chicken could be prepared anyway but fried. And yet, it was an innocent time: One God, one religion, no drugs, no alcohol, no sexual temptations. Boyfriends were well-behaved gentleman and there was an unspoken agreement that sex would wait until marriage. The few that ventured beyond the norm were the 'other kind of kids' — not us. So, without such diversions, high school was for me about learning, acting, making music (cornet and piano), writing bad poetry, riding Mr. Lucky, swimming and high board diving, climbing trees, eating Gram's pies and cobblers, and enjoying pizza and root beer in frosted glasses with my friends. High School also offered the National Honor Society, Latin Club, and being published in a Literary Magazine (1961). Here's one example of an early attempt at haiku:

Small bird, forgive me
I'll hear the end
Of your song
In some other world.

And, of course, there was the music. Mother had insisted when I was twelve that I take piano lessons as that's what Southern ladies do. My teacher's name was Mrs. F. Sharp and she had a three-legged black cat. I was always impressed how that cat could run and climb trees as well as any four-legged feline. For three years, I labored at the piano, hating it more each year. My room was upstairs and Mother was downstairs, insisting I practice. Knowing her to be listening, I would set whatever novel I was engrossed with on the piano where you place music sheets. Then as I kept reading, I would either play scales over and over or a piece I had already learned by heart.

I did end up with a love of music though. I had played the cornet since junior high and had been chosen for regional and all state bands in high school, receiving a school lettered jacket like the football players wore. I was also offered a full scholarship to North Texas State University which had a fine music school. Our band won first prizes everywhere. Mainly, all those hours practicing the horn probably kept me out of trouble. My senior year I was first chair cornet in the All State Band in Denton at North Texas State University at the same time I was playing the female lead in Noel Coward's *Blithe Spirit*. I had to commute back and forth. At the end of *Blithe Spirit*, Ruth Condomine dies and returns as a ghost with white hair. As there was no time to wash the spray dye out of my hair, I had to play the public concert with white hair!

All I cared about was reading and being outside. I loved climbing up the huge mulberry tree and lying against a branch, picking juicy ripened black mulberries and eating them as I read chapter after chapter of *Wuthering Heights*, *Jane Eyre* or other great romances — or *Pilgrim's Progress* which was a major spiritual discovery for me in those early formative years. At age twelve, I loved *Gone with the Wind* so much that the very moment I finished reading the thousand-page novel, I turned back to page one and read the entire book a second time!

As a high school graduation present, I flew with Mother to New York for the first time, and saw several amazing Broadway plays. 1961 was still enjoying the golden Broadway years. Within one week, I saw Uta Hagen (later my acting teacher) in Edward Albee's *Who's Afraid of Virginia Woolf?*, Genet's *The Blacks* directed by Jose Quintero (who would later work with me on a proposed Broadway production of my first long play, *On the Edge: the final years of Virginia Woolf*), Osborne's *Luther* starring the one and only Albert Finney, Jean Anouilh's *The Rehearsal,* and *The Fantasticks* (the longest running off-Broadway musical written by two former drama students of the University of Texas). Though we had tickets to see the new musical, *Stop the World, I Want to Get Off,* my psyche could not take in any more. My cup was running over and my nervous system could not process one more great production. (Later, in 1970 when I returned to New York to professionally pursue acting, the theatre's golden age had sadly passed.)

Winning a National Merit Scholarship, I opted to go to

Phillips University in Oklahoma where missionaries were trained by the Christian Church. My vow was to become an educational missionary in foreign lands. Looking back now, I suspect that I was unduly influenced by the several religious books and Hollywood movies such as *The Ten Commandments*, *Ben Hur, Quo Vadis*, and *The Silver Chalice*. And I was told I looked like Jean Simmons — who one day I would meet in Philadelphia when we were in separate shows on the way to Broadway.

Catherine, age 17

I wrote a short play, *Always a Tomorrow*, in high school, about a prostitute. (No one ever told me to write about what I knew.) Three years later in university — though I never took a class in writing — I wrote two more plays. The first was a play set in an asylum, *Somewhere-in-Between* that had one character speak in poetry, using those ghastly, early poems of mine. (Good to know that nothing is ever lost when you're a writer! All experience — both perceived and written down — might one day be of use somewhere.) *Somewhere-in-Between,* set in an insane asylum, was later produced off-Broadway in New York, receiving a rave review from *The New York Times.* The only other play I wrote while in college, *A Fairy Tale for Adults,* was also professionally produced at the Dallas Theater Center, a wonderful theater designed by Frank Lloyd Wright. This play was about a young girl of eight who ran away because the world is cruel. She meets another runaway, a middle-aged man in the mountains who confirms life's cruelty by his actions.

First love came when I turned fourteen. The attraction was instant. Glen, twenty-one, was my ninth-grade science teacher. It was Glen's first year to teach. I learned later that he was a descendant of the British painter, Sir Joshua Reynolds. Glen was blonde and blue-eyed; I had dark brown hair and brown eyes like my Celtic forebears. We were in love from afar and, of course, good Christians both, it was never consummated. My infatuation with Glen seemed passionately hopeless, and having a tendency toward drama from an early age, one day, I walked into the science lab at school, and came close to drinking a poisonous substance. Fortunately, another student interrupted my considered action and I lived. (Years later, in New York, when I played Juliet in *Romeo and Juliet*, I made good use of 'that moment'. I knew exactly how another fourteen-year-old — that is, Juliet — passionately felt before she took the poison!) Happily, later during that ninth-grade year, I learned that Glen felt the same about me when after school in a dark hallway, we kissed once and vowed to wait. We waited three years, until the day after I graduated high school. On our first date, Glen asked me to marry him. Having committed to become an educational missionary, I asked if he would join me in this, and he said he would. And he generously agreed to wait until I finished college as well.

Informally engaged, Glen and I continued to date throughout the summer sans consummation. Glen introduced me to scuba diving, something we both enjoyed. At summer's end, putting God first, I flew to Enid, Oklahoma to study theology and prepare for my calling. The problem was that during my freshman year at Phillips University. I read and thought too much. I read the world's great religions as well as both eastern and western philosophy. From my journal that same year, I wrote: "In the midst of education, I thirst for Knowledge."

Suddenly, I no longer believed in one god, one religion, but rather a projection of something greater that was always felt within — if not yet known: 'One Light, Many Lamps' as Rumi wrote. Something I had first discovered at age four, standing before the Kamakura Buddha in Japan. So, I knew I must find another college major — and career. And the year had lessened my infatuation with Glen as well. He was no longer the forbidden fruit which may have played a part in becoming infatuated with him at age fourteen.

I competed for Phillips University in the intramural swimming and diving, winning three swimming races (breast-stroke, crawl, and back stroke) plus the high board diving. Also competed in intramural table tennis. Usually I won, but my first competitor was a girl from China. Puzzled that she stood so far back from the table to serve, I soon learned why. Her serve flew by like a torpedo! And I was out of the competition just as fast.

I had played all the female leads in the school plays that year at Phillips U. so decided to transfer to Austin, to The University of Texas as their drama school was #1 in America. In so doing, I approached the theatre with the same religious fervor I had earlier invested in organized religion. Only now, Thespis was the new god.

> I smiled that night,
> For they did not know
> That a cloud passing the moon
> Was naught but the wink of God.

Journal, 1962

The summer after Phillips University, my pragmatic mother insisted I attend a business school in Dallas to learn typing. Finding it tedious and extremely boring, I would sneak out of class and find my way to Theatre Three in downtown Dallas. (Later I would teach myself to type. Because of this subterfuge, I still cannot type numbers well.)

Originally Theatre Three was the Margo Jones Theatre, a theatre started by the Texas fireball, Margo Jones, who launched the first productions of plays by Tennessee Williams: *The Glass Menagerie* and *Summer and Smoke*. I was eighteen when I first entered Theatre Three and met Norma Young, a 'no nonsense' artistic director. I told her I wanted to be in the theatre. She responded, "The johns need cleaning." So, my first job in the theatre was cleaning the toilets!

Soon I was prop mistress for *Sabrina Fair* (Audrey Hepburn, an idol of mine, played her in the Hollywood film, *Sabrina*). The only problem in doing the props for this show was that one prop was 'alive'. It was a large and noisy white cockatoo who was prone to bite the hand that fed it and which I had to take home nightly. Later that summer, I was finally cast as the ingénue in Moliere's *The Doctor in Spite of Himself* and could actually perform! It was one of those 'coming home' experiences — a feeling you have when you meet someone or arrive at some place you feel you already know. Or something like swimming or drawing. (Years later in my second book, *Heal Your Self with Writing,* I would create the *Coming Home* exercise.) Acting was a 'coming home' experience for me, that deep-rooted feeling that "I have done this before."

Through my association with the Dallas theatre, I also came to know T. R. who was ten years my senior. T. R. was both directing and playing one of the two leading roles in Samuel Beckett's now classic play, *Waiting for Godot.* I would hide in a corner and observe rehearsals. One day, T. R. approached and we seemed to hit it off. By this time, I had ended the informal and unconsummated engagement with Glen, my former science teacher. T. R. and I began going out, and by the end of the summer, I was no longer a virgin. What a relief that was! Afterwards, I laughed and said to my now lover, "Is that all?" Meaning, "What's all the hullaballoo, sex is the most natural thing in the world." T.R. was not only an actor, but a fine director, and also a television writer, writing episodes for such Hollywood shows as *Gunsmoke* and other one-hour dramas. T. R. wanted to marry me and I told him that I wanted to first complete my college degree. Mother was fine about the engagement as long as I waited until I was twenty-one. (T.R.'s father was a prominent Dallas banker and I suspect that pleased her, as well.)

Come September, I began my sophomore year at The

University of Texas Austin in the Drama Department. For the next three years, T. R. and I remained engaged. For almost a year, he lived in Morelia, Mexico writing for various Hollywood television series and writing long, wonderfully descriptive letters to me about the annual celebration of the Day of the Dead. He invited me to join him in Mexico, but I declined. I had found my calling in drama and it consumed me entirely: classes by day, rehearsals most nights. We did manage some clandestine weekends in Dallas and Austin though. And when his father died, I caught a Greyhound to Dallas and stayed with him — unknown to my family. He was patient, kind, talented, and he loved the theatre as much as I did — and he was a good lover. I wrote of him in my journal, "He lived life as if it were some private joke he alone understood. Maybe it was." About this time, I began to ponder if it is possible to ever entirely know another. This would later become a theme in my plays and movies.

> Love may be there but comprehension rarely.
> There is nothing to say for we each write our own story and live it accordingly.

> Journal, 1963

Summer of 1963

After my first year in Drama School, I was invited to play the female leads in three plays in summer stock with the *Gaslight*

Players. No salary, only bed and board. So, along with my best friend, Judith, who would play smaller roles and be my understudy, we flew to Estes Park, Colorado for our first acting jobs. Jackie Cooper, the former Hollywood child star, was the producer, Joe Hill, director, and Bill Baker, pianist and songwriter-composer. They brought to Estes Park an intense whiff of Hollywood. I wrote in my journal of Bill Baker who exuded sexuality:

> His casual, sensual movements and warm eyes
> Breathe the promise of love.
> The animal is lonely;
> Its cries are human.
>
> Journal 1963

Of course, nothing happened with Bill as I was still engaged to T.R. who was still living in Mexico. Still, both Judy and I adored sexy Bill. Admittedly, Judy, two years older, was more advanced in that area. Judy, a free spirit, had gotten into some bother at school for posing nude for a *Playboy* magazine centerfold. That long summer, I simply mooned from afar for Bill and worked hard memorizing the leading roles in three plays to be performed in rotation once they had all opened. Our first production was *Angel Street* (*Gaslight* movie with Ingrid Bergman and Charles Boyer) and I was asked to play the Ingrid

Bergman role. A convert to Stanislavski (*An Actor Prepares*), during one rehearsal I went too far playing madness and lost control. The director had to come up and slap me hard. Joe Hill scolded, "Play the part but never, never lose control." I never made that mistake again.

The next leading role was in *The Tender Trap*, a romantic comedy which was made into a film starring Frank Sinatra and Debbie Reynolds. Light but fun. Lastly an original musical melodrama — the name escapes me. I think Bill wrote the music and perhaps the whole musical. As the lead and ingénue, I had to sing for the first time in a musical. This was my biggest challenge though I had sung in church choirs and daily in the shower, my voice was totally untrained. What I remember most of all was the sheer terror of it, especially when singing solo downstage center facing the audience, blinded by a white spotlight which totally blurred seeing the audience or indeed anything else!

One evening after a show, I heard a folk trio perform in a night spot next to the theatre. It was similar to the then popular Kingston trio. The lead singer, a seminary student who planned a career as a minister, invited me for a hike the next day. All three shows were now opened, and as we were given our first day off, I readily accepted the date. I'll call him Rob which might have been his name. Rob was handsome, clean-cut, and a professional mountain climber to boot. My mistake was in saying I had experience mountain climbing when I had none. (Dallas is rather void of mountains.) I did have an adventurous spirit and after working hard for two months rehearsing three shows, was ready for just about anything. Rob explained that you usually had to have permission to climb this mountain as it was considered dangerous. And, as we only dressed to hike, the decision to climb Long's Peak, the second tallest Rocky Mountain in the Estes Park area, was both a spontaneous and risky venture. (My motto then was "I'll try anything once.") Dressed in shorts and a tee shirt, we began the climb — my first mountain as it happened. Sitting atop, the view was glorious, the sun shone down on us as a blessing, and Rob kissed me for the first time, our heads almost touching the clouds. Romance was in the air — but not for long.

All was right with the world — that is, until we started back down. What I did not yet know was that the most challenging part of mountain climbing is the descent. At one point, Rob, though an experienced climber, took forever negotiating his move as there was no clear foothold. Lacking his trained patience, I quickly and haphazardly followed, slipping then free-falling straight down, three-hundred feet! I remember hitting the side of the mountain twice and at last arriving with a thud on a fallen pine tree and hard ground. It took Rob some

41

time to reach me, he just kept shouting, "Don't move. Don't move." Once there, he checked and said that I had broken my ankle, many bleeding abrasions, and might have other internal injuries. I was to wait, not moving, while he climbed down and found the Rangers who would return and rescue me.

Time passed slowly. I recalled my experience immediately after I slipped and began to fall. I remembered that I had asked inwardly, "Is this it?" meaning would I die? The answer came clear and firm: "No, it is not yet finished" meaning I had not yet completed what I came here to do. Reassured, I completely relaxed and experienced a kind of ecstasy in surrendering to the free fall. Later the doctor in the Denver hospital said that's probably what saved me, falling like a cat. The day before my accident, a twenty-one-year old man fell from that very same mountain and was killed instantly. Thus, my first great lesson of the value of surrender.

The other thing I remember vividly while I lay there for some hours waiting for the Rangers was what an absolutely splendid day it was. Birds were singing, white billowing clouds rolling by, a blazing sun shining without the slightest regard for my predicament. This was a humbling realization as well a good life lesson. Whatever happens, life goes on.

Thirteen rangers returned with Rob and they strapped me into a cot with ropes. Then they slowly belayed me down the mountain first to a ranger station where they applied some iodine on my many cuts and abrasions. I knew I was still alive as this hurt like hell. I remember asking for a mirror which they were hesitant to show me. I insisted so finally, I saw myself in the mirror, a face with multiple deep cuts and bleeding gashes. Unless I starred in horror films, I surmised my acting career was probably over. I was placed in an ambulance, lying flat on my back inches from the roof, said goodbye to Rob — not a very promising first date! —, and was driven to St. Anthony's hospital in Denver.

Joe Hill, my director, was furious as we had just opened the three shows and I was his leading lady — now with multiple injuries including a broken ankle. Void of compassion, he told me over the phone, "You're fired!" Show biz. My head demanded eighteen stitches. The X-Rays showed that I had also bruised my spleen and kidney. The broken ankle was put into a cast. My head was sewn up. The multiple cuts and abrasions administered with vitamin E ointment. Meanwhile back at the Gaslight Players, Judy stayed on for the remaining month, took over my roles — and began an affair with sexy Bill!

My mother and stepfather flew up to Denver and carried me home to recover for the month before my junior year began in Austin. (Mother had married Harry during my senior year in high school. I was happy for her as the timing was right, just before the empty nest.) Now back in Texas, I actually enjoyed having nothing to do but to lie around, read, and recover for a full month. Happily, after several weeks of Vitamin E ointment, there was no scarring on face or body. Angel on my shoulder! And the acting career still loomed on the horizon.

Small bird descends
On dreary day
Smile lights unhappy face
Thank you, little friend.

Journal 1963

The Heisters

My junior year, I acted in my first film, *The Heisters,*

directed by Tobe Hooper. I played the role of a dancing girl throwing rose petals in this spoof on horror films. It was a half-hour film in Cinemascope and Technicolor and played on the same bill with *Zorba the Greek* (Anthony Quinn and Alan Bates). It was rather magical for the first time being up on the big screen. A short time later, Tobe asked me to play the main role in his first feature film, *Texas Chainsaw Massacre* (a huge hit!), but I declined as the gore was a bit too much. Later, Tobe went to Hollywood and directed *Poltergeist* (1982) and other scary films — all thankfully without me!

> The scholar at heart,
>
> The actress at will,
>
> The human being incidentally.
>
> Journal, Oct 1963

Inspired by our superb dancing teacher, Shirlee Dodge who had been a professional dancer in Germany with the renown pioneer, Mary Wigman who pre-dated Martha Graham, I was considering majoring in Modern Dance instead of acting. This was not to be due to the climbing accident in the Rockies when I broke my ankle. Shirlee Dodge advised me to stick to the acting.

In September 1963 the Drama Dept invited Hume Cronyn and Jessica Tandy to come and talk to us. Hume was a well-known character actor in films of Alfred Hitchcock and his wife, Jessica Tandy, the original Blanche DuBois in the Pulitzer Prize winning play, *A Streetcar Named Desire* by Tennessee Williams. I remember Cronyn talking about what makes an actor a success, and saying, "It's not even the most talented. It's the most committed."

Some years later through mutual friends, I would meet them again in New York when they were on Broadway in the two-character hit, *The Gin Game*. Hume would take me out for dinner and surprise me by telling me he had a glass eye (from a bout with cancer) and would I like him to take it out. I quickly demurred, saying, "Please, not during dinner." Several years later, Hume Cronyn would beautifully play the lead role in *Angel Passing,* a film I co-wrote with the director, that went on to garner fifteen awards in festivals both here and abroad. (Teresa Wright with whom I had acted in the Broadway revival of Arthur Miller's *Death of a Salesman*, would play Cronyn's wife in our film.)

November 22, 1963. The day America lost its innocence. President Kennedy was shot in Dallas, fifteen minutes from where I grew up. I was struggling in Scene Design Class in Austin when it happened. A nation in limbo. I kept wondering when I would awake and find that this was only a bad dream.

T. R., now back in Dallas, drove down to Austin and we spent two days together in a kind of daze. Watching the brutal and surreal story unfold on television, the continuous replay of the actual shooting of the President then Lee Harvey Oswald shot. Confusion. Chaos. Isn't this America anymore? History cannot be realized until it is past. Sadly now, what was then an unthinkable act is today a common occurrence.

Both my junior and senior year, I began cutting classes and reading, writing, and watching Ingmar Bergman films. After writing *A Fairy Tale for Adults,* I wrote another play, *Somewhere-in-Between* later produced at the Cubiculo Theatre in New York. Mostly, I read voraciously, books 'not' required in my classes. Shall I read this life away? Yes, please!

> When shall I at last return unto solitude alone,
>> without companion,
> without joy and sorrow, with only a sacred
>> certainty that all is a dream?
>
> Kazantzakis, *Zorba the Greek*

Dallas 1964

> On the Road again,
>> Seeing places that I've never seen
>
> Willie Nelson

I was invited through B. Iden Payne the following summer to act in summer stock at the Ashland Shakespeare

Festival in Oregon. (Former students of B. Iden Payne originated the Ashland Shakespeare Theater as well as The Globe Theatre in San Diego, California.) Tough choice but I opted to visit Europe instead because I had never gone there before.

Though leaving home and travelling alone was not new to me, an altogether different feeling accompanied this journey, one of losing hold of one rope in order to grasp another — that final tie with home and childhood which had, until now, seemed to cling forever. A gypsy soul, though my family urged me to join a tour group, I insisted on going solo. In those days, you could book an open airline ticket to as many cities as you wished, deciding at the last minute how long you would stay in each place. Hard to imagine today! For my first trip to Europe, I chose to be away for two whole months dividing the time, as the spirit moved, between Brussels, London, Paris, Munich, Vienna, Venice, Florence, and Rome.

Both my grandparents as well as Mother came to see me off at the Dallas Love Field Airport. Having just turned twenty, I was eager to fly —both metaphorically and physically — yet there they stood as if at a funeral saying goodbye to me for the possibly last time. My mother had asked for a gold coin for her charm bracelet and my grandmother asked for a spoon for her collection. When I asked my grandfather what he would like from Europe, he simply said, "I just want you to come back." My grandmother gave me a red carnation from her garden, saying it is a flower of love. Two hours later on the flight, the carnation began to wilt. I didn't mind, for I knew that only the flower would wilt. Still, as eager as I was for this pilgrim journey, I felt a twinge of sadness leaving those behind who cared for me. How strange that in the greatest joy can be found some small sadness.

On the way to Europe, I stopped over in New York for three days to visit Jillian Lindig, a former drama student now a professional NY actress. I told Jillian who was two years ahead of me in school that I had been glad to see her graduate so I could begin playing more leading roles at school! She laughed, totally getting it. It was a perfect time to be in New York as the 1964 World's Fair was on. I saw the *Pieta* by Michelangelo and through director Tobe Hooper met a film producer, Charles Lasater. Lasater gave me the name of Aldo Vitali in Rome who wrote screenplays for Antonio's art films. I promised to call him.

It was wonderful to see Jillian's New York and theatre life as this was what I aspired to do after graduation. Decades later, Jillian and her actor-husband, John Michalski, remain close friends, still actors, and still happily married to each other.

Brussels. June 26.

Hello, Europe, I am yours! Strolling down flower-scented

streets. Here the people have time to be happy as they place a priority on living. I watch various dogs running here and there and wonder if they bark a different language, one native to their habitat? Two gentlemen from Morocco attempt Spanish and French to no avail. No matter for even here, a Texas smile goes a long way! Odd how these Europeans, with whom I feel are kindred spirits, respond in kind. However, I confess that I prefer the Americans abroad in small dosages. They are often loud and always in such a hurry while I stay on drinking tea and chatting with waiters.

London. June 27.

57 Pont Street, Swan Square, Knightsbridge. A small B&B with a window overlooking London's cobblestone roads and Victorian red brick houses. Window boxes sprout red geraniums, violets, Sweet Williams — all brilliant colors. Streetlights unchanged for the last hundred and fifty years, very British.

Lunch with Suzy Chan, twenty-nine, a very beautiful, six-foot high fashion model, and a former Miss Hong Kong in the Miss Universe contest. When Suzy was twelve, her family lost everything to the Chinese Communists. She is soon to play a supporting role to Sophia Loren in *Imperial Woman*. She knows everyone who is anyone. Time and money are no problem for Suzy as she is being kept by an American Embassy Pictures mogul. Pepe, her toy Scottish terrier, was a gift from actor Dan Dailey in Acapulco. They are great friends, being gay so having the same sexual orientation in common. Suzy loves name-dropping of her friends such as Sammy Davis, Jr., Warren Beatty and his sister, Shirley MacLaine. Lunch at Camden Towers with two very well-to-do Englishmen — pleasant if a bit stuffy. They insist that I join them in the south of France, a favorite playground for the jet set. Jonathan's family is what Woolworth is to the States. He is also a descendant of actress Ellen Terry though his business is making helicopters. He and his friend, Robert, invite me to join them for dinner after my theatre plans this evening but I decline. Tonight, the first of five nights at the London theatre, a priority for my first London stay.

Five hours flew by at the sprawling British Museum. My soul travelled back many thousands of years. I saw a man over five thousand years old, his body still on this earth. The Shabako Stone, a text of ancient drama, 700 B.C., made from an older document on papyrus in 3000 B.C., the beginning of the dynastic period. I am fascinated by the ancient mummies who lived before 3500 B.C. Met and lunched with an anthropology professor from Sweden who is here writing another book. I return to the British Museum in order to view original manuscripts of Shakespeare, Goethe, Dickens, Jonson, Racine, Wagner, Schumann, Joyce, Shaw. Saw also the Magna Charta and the Wycliffe Bible. Seeing the Elysian Marbles, the sculpture relief from the Parthenon in Athens. Electric! I watch as Lapith and the Centaur fight a mighty battle. I saw the bottomless eyes of Homer who seemed to see more than most. I wondered why Aristophanes was not laughing, and determined to reread them all!

National Gallery for two and a half hours: Da Vinci. Rubens. Turner. Van Dyck. Titian. Veronese. Goya. Monet. Van Gogh. Michelangelo. Van Eyck. Holbein. There are no words of the depths these images excite. Only a profound silence can prove an adequate response. Travelling alone is a wonderful adventure as you meet so many interesting people, listen to their stories, and before you know it, the portals of your provincial mind open wide, expanding to limitless horizons.

Stratford-on-Avon

Either accidently or intuitively I was led to one of the loveliest churches I have ever seen. I sometimes miss the innocent faith of childhood. Buddha. Christ. Did I embrace a patriarchal god to replace an absentee father? Cruel intellect demolished the inherited walls of organized religion forever. Wisdom stands alone, a tall and lonely tower.

Unexpectedly inside the church, I chanced upon the grave of William Shakespeare, with these words engraved in stone:

Good friend for Jesus sake forebeare

To dig the dust enclosed heare,

Bless be the man who spares these stones

And curst be he who moves my bones.

Before me burns an old candle, which hangs from a
wooden beam

At least four hundred years old. Burn sweet candle. Burn while I mutter my prayer to an unknown god. I find peace with antiquity, ever at home with the dead, yet only a distant understanding of the living.

Journal, 1964

Paris. July 12

I arrive in Paris on the eve of Bastille Day, July 13. Oh, to possess the tongues of all this world so that wherever I go, I might truly know the people, the portal to the heart of any country.

My hotel room looked more like a brothel though tastefully done in passionate red and white wallpaper. Comedie-Francaise to see Edmund Rostand's play, *Cyrano de Bergerac*. Tradition pre-curtain three knocks with staff announcing that the play is about to commence. The spectacle of sixty actors on stage in the first scene and a carriage with two white horses was a definite highlight.

Rive Gauche

Purchased mid-nineteenth century editions of Voltaire, Corneille, Victor Hugo in a Left Bank rare bookstore. Walking by the Seine, observing a myriad of wine corks drifting by in a river that does not flow, wondering what tales of love or woe each cork holds?

An evening of Ionesco's short plays, *The Lesson* and *The Bald Soprano*. These absurd writings seem far more real somehow than today's more conventional plays.

An evening of Samuel Beckett's short plays, one was fifteen minutes long and without words! I smiled discovering from the program that I was born on Beckett's birthday.

I can only estimate my work from within.

Samuel Beckett

Firenze (Florence) Aug 1964

City of dreams. Straw Market. I buy the world! I bargain for an old wooden hand-painted globe from the artisan who took me back to his studio to find one without chipped paint. We did and he will post it home for me — which, thankfully, he did! Dinner at a bistro of noodle soup, pulled beef and mashed potatoes, and vin rouge. Delicious and cheap!

Michelangelo's *David* must be seen to be believed. What struck me was the oversized hand in comparison with the body, this the hand that slew Goliath.

The next morning, leaving my pensione next to the Duomo in the center of Florence, I begin to walk, no map, no plan or destination. The sun's warmth my protector. I reach the outskirts of town and stroll along a hillside vineyard where lush, ripened grapes abound. Hungrily I pluck the grapes, eating them under the sensual Italian sun, then lay down for a nap, the vibrant vines shading me. Twenty minutes later, I awake and continue to walk and walk and walk. I come to an old cemetery with the iron gate locked. I pull the antiquated bell and soon a wizened guard, stooped from labor, comes to let me in. Sometimes an intuitive feeling takes over and guides. This was such a moment as I am pulled to a particular grave. A lovely green bough bends over the tombstone. I stoop to read the stone when suddenly an unexpected breeze comes, causing white petals from surrounding rosebushes to fall upon my head and hands. At first, I think it has begun to rain then realize that they are white, rose petals blown by the breeze descending as Love's tears from above. I read the stone: "Grave of Elizabeth Barrett Browning 1806-1861." She was fifty-five. I think of Robert Browning buried in Westminster Abbey, London, and regret that these lovers have been parted in death. I feed a small turtle that has made of her grave his or her home. I am thanked by turtle urine running across my hand. There is no inscription or verse upon her stone — only her name and dates. How could there be when her very life was poetry. A passage from the Bible comes to mind which I recite out loud as I commune with this lovely poet lying alone in an abandoned graveyard:

> Neither can they die anymore.
> For they are equal unto the angels.
>
> Luke 20:36

Sorrento

A lovely small town where I am scheduled to catch the boat to Capri. While waiting, I sit at an outdoor café for a cup of tea, joined by a handsome older man I take for a worker as he is casually dressed in shorts and a sleeveless white t-shirt. He turns out to be the mayor of Sorrento! Later, I purchase a small wooden marquetry inlaid table that when opened, plays *The Isle of Capri*. The shipped table will await my return to Texas.

Isle of Capri

The small, leisurely boat carries me to the living myth known as the Isle of Capri. Gentle showers fall as I hire a horse and cart up the steep hill to the top of the mountain, the expanding vista taking my breath away. I arrive at a posh resort hotel and decide to have lunch there on the patio, the rain having stopped.

An American woman of thirty-five years, beckons to me to join her for lunch. Vera's father is the president of one of America's largest corporations. She is attractive, six feet tall, wearing white silk pants, leather beach heels, blue jersey pull over with a matching blue silk scarf binding her long brown unkept hair. On her finger displaying the largest diamonds I had ever seen and her ears, gold leaf earrings with small diamond centers. She holds in her hand an elegant small ivory cigarette holder which on occasion, she waves for emphasis. I sit down at her invitation and am introduced to a young Italian couple in their early twenties who did not seem to understand English. Toward the end of lunch, she waves the young couple away as one would a waiter. Vera then leans over after lighting her cigarette and in a hushed voice, asks if I would like to join her in an afternoon's entertainment. She explains that the young couple who had just left the table will make love in her room as she watches. She has paid them two hundred dollars to perform the act. Perverse entertainment. I say no to the after-lunch entertainment then walk along the cliff letting the gentle sea air wash over me.

A taste of wealth is a very dangerous thing. I observe this in others on this trip but wonder why wealth has never been a temptation for me. I seek beauty, art, knowledge, even Truth. Never wealth. But then I am but twenty and for the moment, the whole world is mine!

Roma

Roma, Roma, how do I love thee? Let me count the ways…

Castle of the Angels, Hadrian's Tomb

I am happy these idyllic Roman days. Happiness is simple. Solitude, a treasured luxury. I sit and meditate until a white uniformed policeman bids me move on lest robbers beat me and steal my purse!

Harry's Bar, Rome

I sit with a ginger ale with actor Trevor Howard who is in Rome filming *The Bible* in which he portrays Abraham. I am mesmerized by his lined face of a life lived intensely — if not wisely.

Café de Paris on Via Veneto

Met by chance the one and only Frank Sinatra. He is charming though tipsy and displays a violent temper when a paparazzi, without permission, takes his photograph. Sinatra has a small scar on one side of his face and always makes sure it is never seen in photos. He attacks the photographer and a frightening fight ensues. Later, he invites me to his villa to a party he is hosting. I decline.

The Appian Way, Catacombs, & St. Sebastiano

The next day, I walk the Appian Way, the ancient Roman road not far from Rome. I take a large chunk of cheese, baguette freshly baked, and a small roll of salami. The more I walk the stronger the sensation that I have walked these roads before. I come across the St. Sebastiano Catacombs where, fearing Roman persecution, early Christians hid — only their skulls remaining, gazing aimlessly at all who pass by.

Later not far from the monastery, I find a cave carved from a gigantic stone set in the middle of a sprawling pasture. I enter the large, dark cave and psychically begin to relive another time long ago, hiding in this same cave, fearing the Roman soldiers. Ancient memories haunt as I, an early Christian, fear persecution, evoking the traumatic memory of another life. I cannot explain this but it is so. Fear overwhelms as I crouch down and crawl on all fours to the back of the cave. Then I become absolutely still, hardly breathing as though my life depended on it. It did, once. Unaware of how much time has passed, I finally take a huge breath and again silently resume walking the Appian Way, pondering unexplained mysteries.

A Roman Holiday

Charles Lasater whom I had met in New York had suggested I look up screenwriter Aldo Vidali while in Rome. I call him on my third day in Rome and half an hour later we are sitting together at Café de Paris on the Via Veneto. Aldo Vidali, 34, is a screenwriter and artist who works with the famed Italian director, Michelangelo Antonioni (*La Notte,* 1961, starring Marcello Mastroianni and Monica Vitti.) His writing nom de plume is Charles Henry Wilde while he paints under Henry Wilde. The illegitimate son of a Belgium opera singer and an Italian father, Aldo is handsome, charming, full of 'Le Dolce Vita'. On our first day together, he drives me to several sites in Rome including the Vatican and a Punch and Judy show in a local park. Dinner at a lovely outdoor café in the Piazza with white wine, stimulating conversation, and red roses bought from a passing gypsy woman. Later Aldo shows me his own paintings in his large, marble-floored apartment. They are excellent art yet I leave soon after as he becomes a bit too charming after the wine!

The next day, we are off to the beaches at Astoria not far from Rome. Aldo knows of a private beach belonging to Marquis somebody. We swim in the Mediterranean, salt kisses in the sea. Sharing one towel as we lie on the beach warmed by the sun. Back to Rome to Aldo's marbled-floor flat to what seems inevitable, love in the afternoon. After making love, I remember Aldo sitting naked on rumpled white sheets with his guitar, playing and singing an Italian love song.

"Aldo, I want to be many things to you. More than a body."

"Catherina, you are a body to my body, a mind to my mind, a soul to my soul. Don't be a mind to my body."

Aldo laughs as he tells me that he has been chosen for a dukedom. We visit Meapataco, a tiny 16th-17th century village, full of colored lanterns which hang throughout the courtyard. A white horse and rider ride up and down the street all evening. The happiness of the people eating and drinking outside is contagious. A singer with guitar and clarinet, tuba, trumpet, tapirine, recorder, and bamboo flute serenade us all. Wagons of wine pass frequently. Now everyone is singing in the candle light. The Balloon man comes holding large colorful balloons with long, long strings. Here come children of all ages to buy them. Presto as the piazza is studded with red, blue, yellow and green balloons launched from the empty wine bottles atop the tables. Roma, city of over a million yet still a village at heart! How free and joyful are these wonderful people who know how to live. I feel as if my heart will burst! The idyllic days continue with Aldo as if in a dream. A lovely dream but a dream all the same. But eventually, one must awake.

Earlier today, I had declined an offer to act in a film soon to be shot at Cinecitta Studios, the largest film studio in Europe. Rome has become too intense for this Texas gal just turned twenty. A kind of lethargy dominates the eternal city and it frightens me. Tonight, I resolve to leave Rome and return to complete my final year at school. Aldo. I don't know if I can say good bye to Aldo. Yet I feel strongly that if I don't leave tomorrow, I may become one of those American drifters that live on for years and years, and only speak of returning home.

The next morning, as if an alarm sounded within, the sudden decision to flee Rome's magical hold and complete my senior year at university is confirmed. I have awakened from the Roman dream. I call Aldo to say I am flying home and thank him for an unforgettable Roman holiday. Yes, I shall fly away but with what memories packed away within! Thank you, Roma!

A trip to Europe can be many things to many people. Each must find his own Europe, his own Paris, his own Roma, his own separate self. I am but twenty yet feel as if there is nothing in the world that is not mine! The trick is not to want to own it — only to remember.

Austin, Texas, 1964-5

Rapunzel and the Witch

My senior year begins at The University of Texas. I am cast in many leading roles including the scary witch in *Rapunzel and the Witch.*

The first performance my 'witch' was so terrifying that

two children ran screaming out the door. So, Dr. Jennings, my director, told me to "Bring it down a bit."

This next year will be a preparation to become a professional actor. Soon I was cast as Karen in *The Children's Hour* by Lillian Hellman (also born in New Orleans). After a performance, I found a note addressed to me on the bulletin board. It read, "An excellent performance. Please see me in my office. B. Iden Payne." Thrilled, I timidly knocked on his door. And so it was that I had the great pleasure of working with B. Iden Payne, former director of Stratford-on-Avon in England, now a professsor, eighty-three years young! Mr. Payne began working with me privately on voice and interpretation of Shakespeare, and would cast me in a major role in the upcoming production of Shakespeare's *Measure for Measure.* Payne knew every word of Shakespeare by heart so never had to look at a script. If you missed a single word, he would interrupt the rehearsal, "Excuse me, isn't there a 'the' before that line?"

Iambic Pentameter ruled the day. Payne was both mentor and director, and later after my marriage, became a dear friend to both my husband and me.

Measure for Measure

After being cast in Shakespeare's *Measure for Measure*, two of my friends talked me into going to Selma for the great march for civil rights. However, here's the rub. Mr. Payne made it clear that no rehearsals could be missed or you would be replaced. This became a major turning point for me. I stayed up the entire night trying to choose between two passions: marching in Selma or Shakespeare. Shakespeare or Selma? Early the next sleepless morning, the decision was made. I chose Shakespeare, and never looked back.

B. Iden Payne had arranged for a scholarship to RADA (Royal Academy of Dramatic Art in London) so my post-graduation dream of living and working in London was firmly in place.

However, as John Lennon once said, "Life is what happens to you when you're busy making plans." Yet I could never have imagined the unusual course mine would soon take.

PART II Marriage, Motherhood, & Separation
France, Ireland, New York

Love consists of this: two solitudes that meet,

Protect, and greet each other.

Rainer Maria Rilke

One unexpected day a stranger from a strange land appeared in the form of a Brahmin philosopher-novelist from south India, and my world would never be the same again.

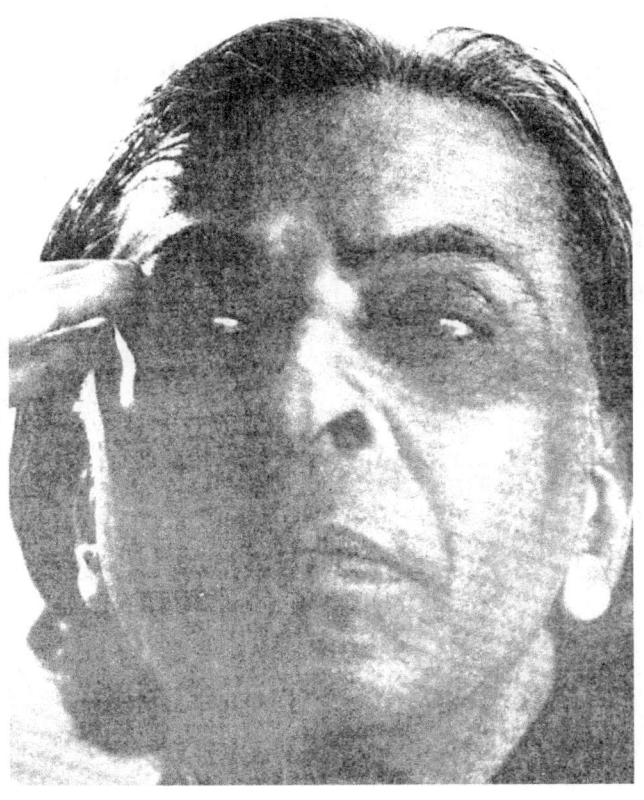

His name was Raja Rao. It all began my junior year just before the magical summer in Europe. It was in Austin, Texas, University of Texas campus, corner of Guadalupe (the main drag) and the Student Union. I had just seen a poster with a striking photo of Raja Rao, guest speaker from India lecturing on *The Way of the Buddha*. One minute later, I stood on the corner and looked up as a car slowly passed and the man sitting in the passenger seat was the same as on the poster. Our eyes locked for one brief moment yet between us, there was a distinct spark of recognition. This was the first time we had seen each other — that is, in this life.

The times they were a changing in the mid-sixties. There was a revolutionary reaction to the presumed value of what could be measured from the outside rather than from inner experience. This began for some a turning to ancient eastern philosophy as exemplified by Harvard professor Richard Alpert, "Ram Dass", in his best-selling book, *Be Here Now*. The young were seeking a 'new reformation', a revival of genuine spiritual experience in the face of a materialistic society. Raja Rao would play his part in this cultural explosion in America.

I had searched since childhood for spiritual answers, leaving organized religion once and for all at age eighteen. Recently Zen Buddhism — so appealing to the Western mind — had drawn me. And now, the mystique of India represented by this remarkable man who had come to the university to deliver ten lectures on eastern philosophy — that is, Hinduism and Buddhism. Unlike today in America, few immigrants from India were visible in the mid-sixties. In fact, Raja Rao was the first east Indian I had ever seen.

For the next ten weeks, I sat at the back of a large packed hall, too shy to ask a single question. I took many notes and felt at last a glimpse of what I had been searching for since age seven. Purchasing two novels authored by Raja Rao, I was especially drawn to his philosophical novel, *The Serpent and the Rope*. Reading it made me feel that I already knew this book. I was to learn much later that the Swedish Secretary General of the United Nations who was awarded the Nobel Peace Prize, Dag Hammarskjöld, was the one who first nominated Raja Rao for the Nobel Prize in Literature. I learned that Hammarskjold carried two books with him at all times, *The Bible* and *The Serpent and the Rope*. However, I was unaware of Raja's fame until well after we were married.

Ten weeks later, I was at the Public Television Station on campus where I was weekly acting in a children's show called *Tippy and Friends,* a national televised show for small children. There were two main characters: an Emmett Kelly-styled circus clown mime who did not speak and a little girl who did. I was that little girl who lived in an enchanted forest. The theme song, mirroring the times, was "Puff the Magic Dragon". After work, I was leaving the station when I glimpsed that someone in the studio next to ours was interviewing Raja Rao. I stood and watched from the technical booth. Afterwards, I turned to leave when Raja Rao called out to me. This was our first initial meeting. He said that he was leaving Austin tomorrow and there was a dinner party being given by his friend, Kim Taylor, an Art Professor at the University. Would I come? Raja gave me Taylor's number. I called and was formally invited to attend that evening.

Kim and Eya Taylor, who were soon to become my 'home away from home', greeted me warmly at their house in the West Lake Hills in Austin. Their two blonde fairy children danced around us, enchanting all. Kim, an Englishman born in Calcutta and Eya, a kind of earth mother from Zurich, Switzerland, had met Raja in Europe some years before. There were about fifteen guests at the party. It was dusk and most of us sat outside on a ramshackle wooden terrace with an expansive view of the surrounding West Lake Hills. I was seated next to Raja Rao who asked why I had never asked a question as he had noticed the many notes I wrote during his talks in the past ten weeks. "Do you have any questions? If so, ask them now. I leave tomorrow."

"Yes," I answered, "I have seventeen questions." Raja

laughed and echoed, "Seventeen questions!" And so, it began —
a kind of leela or divine play. Somehow the world disappeared.
No one existed except this exotic philosopher, myself, and
seventeen questions. Raja Rao had a magnetic presence. His
eyes were unusual in that a silver/bluish ring encircled each of
his deep dark pupils. When he entered a room, both men and
women would become silent and turn and look at him.

At one point, we looked up, it was totally dark, and no
one was there. That is, no one except the two of us. Time had
passed unawares. The others had discreetly withdrawn and gone
inside, leaving us in deep dialogue. It was time to go. Raja told
me to come the next morning to the Forty Acres Club, the faculty
club where he was staying.

The next morning, skipping class, I walked across
campus to the Forty Acres Club, to his room. Kim and Eya were
there and did not seem surprised to see me. Raja was packing
two suitcases: one with clothes (he always wore the same styled
Indian black suit with a Nehru collar — no tie — and a white
Indian shirt), and inside the other suitcase, books and unfinished
manuscripts. Also, a colorful handknitted purple pullover from
Paris which made his face glow. I asked if he would sign my
copies of two of his novels, *Kanthapura* and *The Serpent and
the Rope* — my personal favorite.

He sat down then and there, took out his pen and signed

both of the books. Here is what he inscribed:

Kanthapura: For Catherine Jones, a preliminary stage of my Indian pilgrimage, this work from Raja Rao — Austin 17.5.64 (May 17, 1964)

"I was born a Brahmin, that is, devoted to the Truth and all that."— *The Serpent and the Rope*, opening sentence

The Serpent and the Rope: For Catherine Jones, this book of pilgrimage that she go beautifully to the end of her pilgrimage, from Raja Rao Austin. 17.5.64 (May 17, 1964)

This did not feel like the beginning of a relationship at all. No, rather it was a continuation of an existing union from long ago. I was nineteen and Raja was fifty-five.

I did not see Raja Rao again for a year including the summer I explored Europe for the first time. I did think of him, wondering if this wandering philosopher might return to Texas. I believe he wrote to me once. And return he did the following year, spring of 1965, again as a guest lecturer. Upon his arrival, he called and this time we met often over dinner with long discussions.

We both expressed the sensation of having always known one another. So, a few weeks later when he asked me to marry him, there was really no decision, no doubt. It was as though our union was already in place as some unstoppable river. One only had to embrace the flow.

The lives of creative people as well as seekers seldom travel in straight lines. Their paths often diverge on what becomes a precarious yet exciting adventure. As said by poet Robert Frost: "Two roads diverged in a village wood and I took the road less travelled — and that has made all the difference."

It was graduation time and Raja met my mother and step-father, Harry, who visited Austin, though they were as yet unaware of the real relationship between us. After graduating, I went home to alert the family of our plan to marry. I told Raja that I would not run away but must tell them first. After telling the family, what I did not know then was that my step-father, Harry, enraged, took a gun and Texas-style, flew to Austin to find and shoot Raja Rao! Fortunately, Raja was not at the faculty club and Harry never found him or shot him. Back in Dallas, my sweet grandmother told me, "You know if you had a child, you could never bring a black child home." My mother said that this marriage would kill my grandfather who had been coping with Parkinson's Disease for many years now. It was pointless to argue that east Indians were not Black but an ancient Aryan race. So, I prepared to simply leave and join my future husband in New York where he awaited me. I remember telling my mother, "You may be right in that the marriage will not last. All I know is that it is true now and if I don't act on what is true at each moment then my whole life is a lie." How simple everything seems at twenty!

After two days in New York City at the Hotel Pierre, we flew to Paris. Raja had moved to Paris at the age of nineteen when he was given a scholarship to the Sorbonne, to study the Albigensian heresy about the Cathars in 13th century France for his doctorate. He had married a French professor ten years his senior and some years later, they had divorced. For the last fifteen years, he had taken a former renowned French beauty for his mistress, fifteen years his senior. A close friend, Albert Jolis, owned the second largest diamond mines in Africa. Originally from Brussels, Bert now lived on Avenue Foch near the Arc de Triumph in Paris. There we stayed. As I recall, Sophia Loren and Carlo Ponti, her producer-husband, lived in the flat below us.

Here's a humorous anecdote about French bureaucracy. There was a problem obtaining a marriage license as Raja had no birth certificate. In the small village in Mysore where he was born, there were no birth certificates. As the clerk said to my fiancé, "Monsieur, how can we permit you to wed when you cannot even prove that you were ever born?" How very French! During this waiting time, George Lillas, a friend of Raja's and a wealthy department store owner, lent us his flat in Grasse, in the south of France. Grasse, a picturesque town between Nice and Cannes, is known for its perfumes. Our expansive flat and wide terrace overlooked the hills and immense flowering bougain-villea. A perfect lover's nest. Here we waited for permission to wed from the tangles of the French government.

During this time, some psychic experiences occurred. I was awakened several nights by a soldier dressed in ancient gear standing at the foot of my bed. He had probably been killed in a battle on this ground centuries before and was suffering. Often, when humans die a violent and sudden death, the soul is unable to move on. So, they often seek those empaths as myself to help them. Raja had been of great help to me in understanding my psychic tendencies and gradually I learned not to fear their varied manifestations.

After two months in a Riviera paradise, we finally received the awaited telegram. Fortunately, Raja knew someone who knew someone in the government, and, after a long though pleasant delay, a way was found to obtain the necessary license to wed. In Paris, I was taken to Place Vendome to choose a wedding ring and found an exquisite gold band in the shape of a

Indian Embassy, Paris, October 1965

solid linked chain. I would wear it for almost twenty years.

A simple wedding at the French Civi was arranged with some of Raja's friends. I knew not one word in French and at one point, Raja leaned toward me and said to say "oui". (I wondered what it was I had said *yes* to!) Bert hired a photographer to take photos.

The wedding reception was held at the Indian Embassy in Paris. Raja's close friend, Rajeshwar Dayal, was then ambassador to France. It was a rather grand affair with not one person or family member of my own. Maggi, my college roommate, did send flowers though. I heard Indian music for the first time in my life as another friend of Raja's played the sitar. His name was Ravi Shankar, along with his amazing tabla player. I wore a sari for the first time, it was a shimmering gold silk and stunning though I remember it kept slipping down over my shoulder! A congratulatory telegram arrived from President Charles de Gaulle acknowledging Raja's service to France in bringing France and India closer together. Raja, through his close friendship with Andre Malraux who was Minister for Cultural Affairs from 1958 to 1969, had travelled with Malraux to India and brought him together with Nehru and his daughter, Indira Gandhi, who years later — as her father had been — would also become Prime Minister of India.

It would be a year after our marriage before I learned that Raja had no money, and in fact had never had a job in his life, though he was fifty-five. The guest lecture appointment at The University of Texas was, in fact, his first employment.

After the Independence of India from Great Britain in 1947, Raja's friend, Jawaharlal Nehru, India's first Prime Minister, offered Raja a job as his personal secretary. Raja asked him what that would mean. Nehru replied, "You would mainly write letters for me. That's about it." Raja refused his friend's offer, saying, "I couldn't do that. It might spoil my writing style." Raja was in his early twenties when his first novel, *Kanthapura,* was published to wide acclaim. It depicts a Gandhian village during the fight for India's independence and is now considered a literary classic in and beyond India. During the crusade for India's independence, M. Gandhi invited Raja to come to his ashram and translate some letters from French to English. He agreed to come with certain conditions. Raja refused to wear 'khadi' (ashram clothing) as he dressed rather fine in those days. He insisted on having coffee daily. And he refused to clean the latrines as everyone in the ashram was expected to do — even Gandhi's wife, Kasturba. Gandhi agreed and Raja served the Mahatma for a year. The others in the ashram intensely resented the special privileges given to Raja Rao.

Three years after we were married and began to travel each year to India with our young son, Indira Gandhi, daughter of Nehru and now Prime Minister of India, invited us for tea at Government House in New Delhi. I remember that though polite, she seemed reserved, shrewd, and curious to figure out why Raja Rao would have chosen an American wife. I had heard that she did not care greatly for Americans. Not long after, in 1984, Prime Minister Gandhi was shot twenty-five times by two of her own Security Staff, members of the Sikh religion. Once again, violence in the name of religion.

After the Paris wedding, we flew to Dublin for a honeymoon in Ireland. Raja had been invited by the *Saturday Review* magazine to write an article about an *Indian Philosopher in Ireland.* Forty percent Irish, I was delighted as I had always wished to visit the home of my ancestors who had travelled to Virginia in the mid-seventeenth century. It was a magical month as we traversed the whole of the Republic of Ireland — and met the still living literary lions: Jack Yeats, Monk Gibbon. Sean O'Faolain invited us to his lovely home and with a twinkle in his eye, told us that he wrote one article for a big American magazine and bought his house with the proceeds. We were not so fortunate but Raja's article gave us ample funds for a memorable month in Ireland.

And I actually saw the little folk! At first, I felt their presence in a small glen just outside Dublin. I knew they were watching though I did not see them then. Later, as we were driving back to Dublin, I had a glimpse of them swaying in the branches of a tree. (I later learned that this was the fairy tree.) They were smaller than I had imagined but just as mischievous, laughing and merrily swaying on the branches. Three years later while living in India with our two-year-old son, I made up a story, *Little Boy Butterfly*, later published as a book for children of all ages.

Actually, our son, Christopher, was conceived in the Shelbourne Hotel in Dublin. I know I'm not the first woman to say it, but I did know, beyond doubt, the moment our son was conceived. Afterwards, my husband and I took a walk on St. Stephen's Green (Park). We saw a small boy playing, about age two, and he came running toward us yet seemed not to see us. We both had an eerie feeling as though this was a premonition of sorts. Moreover, months earlier in Austin before we wed, I had had a waking vision of a son waiting to be born to us, as he would — and did — look at age five. However, these premonitions soon faded from memory as the present was so alive with us.

Two memorable psychic events occurred while in Ireland. One time we chose an open field near town to have a picnic. However, as soon as I stepped upon the ground, I saw blood everywhere. I told Raja we could not eat there. My husband, aware of my psychic abilities, suggested we ask in the village about this meadow. We learned that two hundred years ago, many were killed in an extremely bloody battle.

The second occurrence was at a monastic ruin near Athlone. The monastery dated from the 6th century when founded by St. Ciarin and was set on the River Shannon. I stood near a tall round tower and teleported back to the 9th century, saw a large Viking ship land on the bank with a chieftain and his queen as well as many Viking soldiers. The soldiers slaughtered many monks, raped women, and desecrated the holy chapel. The chieftain placed his queen upon the altar and had her drink wine from a holy chalice. This waking state vision stayed with me for two decades and as a puppy snapping at my heels, would not go away. Twenty-two years later, I sat down in N. California and wrote the story as a screenplay in ten days. It came through me as I felt that I was not the author but merely an instrument. After writing the first draft, I went to a library in Los Angeles to research ninth century Ireland, Viking lore, and monastery life. There I learned that what I saw in the vision had *actually* happened at this particular monastery in the ninth century. Every detail I saw was historical fact!

En route to Paris, we stopped over in London for a few days to visit Raja's UK publisher, John Murray, Ltd., who had also published Lord Byron. Byron's boots were enthroned in a glass box in the lobby! The novelist E. M. Forster was also one of their noted authors and the one who had championed Raja's writings. In fact, when he read *The Serpent and the Rope*, he said to Raja, "If only I had written that." Invited to join Forster for tea, we headed to Kings College, Cambridge University, where Forster lived overlooking the courtyard. He lived simply and boiled water on a hot plate before serving us tea with biscuits. I remember Forster saying, "People are always asking me why I didn't write more novels. It was really very simple. I had nothing more to say." After tea, we walked to the Chapel across from his building and went in. The well-known Boys Choir was practicing and we stood at the back listening. Glorious music. Soon after, I procured three of Forster's novels and read them for the first time: *Room with a View, A Passage to India,* and my personal favorite, *Howard's End.* What I remember most of our day with him was Forster's humility and unassuming kindness.

Back in Paris staying again with Bert and Eva on Ave Foch, I was on an errand alone and fainted in the Metro (subway). Later, carried by the police in a Paddy wagon, I was returned safely to Ave Foch. Eva, who had borne three sons, took me aside and after questioning me, suggested I was most likely pregnant! Her doctor soon confirmed this.

Raja felt called to return to India but wanted me to go ahead to Austin to find us a flat. He had been asked to teach and had been offered a tenured professorship by Dr. John Silber, head of the Philosophy Dept. Silber, who could recite by heart whole passages from Raja's third novel, *The Cat and Shakespeare,* said, "I want to have you here teaching Eastern philosophy as you will be a thorn in the others' side."

Dr. John Silber, chairman of the Philosophy Department, later Chancellor of Boston University, liked to provoke and make people think. A remarkable man in many ways and a good friend.

Dr. John Silber

In the mid-sixties, American youth were just becoming aware of Eastern Philosophy so Hinduism and Buddhism would be his subject. (Later Raja asked me if I would object if he only taught four months a year instead of nine months. Though it meant one half the salary, I said, "Of course, your writing must come first."

I sailed alone on the final voyage of the great luxury liner, *The France*, renowned for its exceptional French cuisine. Alas, I was so sick during early months of the pregnancy, all I could manage was oatmeal porridge — all week! And it was a rough winter crossing which did not help matters.

One afternoon in Austin as I was driving around various homes near campus, somehow, intuitively the right place appeared. It was a sunny apartment over a three-car garage set behind a large two-storied duplex. And it was within walking distance to campus. Raja had never learned to drive a car. As I had been disinherited by my family due to my marriage and Raja had little, I knew we had to be prudent. Though there was no 'For Rent' sign, I strongly felt that this was our place. I boldly rang the bell and a young, nice looking tall, slender man answered. I asked him if by any chance he was giving up this flat. Then, with much surprise, he said, "Yes, I am. But I haven't listed it as yet." His name was Van Cliburn, the Texas pianist soon to be world famous. This is how this lovely flat built from the same limestone quarry that had built the University of Texas Tower Library, became our first home.

2 BR, 1 Bath, a small garden in the back, and a splendid view of the West Lake Hills from what would soon become our son's sunny room. I put up a folding card table covered with a burnt orange silk cloth in the corner of the living room overlooking the back garden, and here Raja would write his award-winning novels. Soon my husband would return to the States and approve of the flat. There was a small dining alcove next to three windows with massive oak trees outside providing shade where we would sit talking for hours — during and after meals. It was

a happy time, and though in the south of France and the voyage home I was very sick for the first three or four months of the pregnancy, from month five on, I felt better than ever before in my entire life.

Nine months after the conception in the Shelbourne Hotel, nearing the time of our son's birth, I made out the birth announcements. I found Japanese rice paper and inked a small drawing then wrote this haiku by Basho:

> Gazing at Falling Petals
> A Baby Almost Looks
> Like a Buddha.

Lastly, I added my 'still to be born' son's name: Christopher Rama Rao. Christopher for Ireland and Rama as the main character in Raja's autobiographical novel, *The Serpent and the Rope*. Friends teased how could I possibly know it would be a boy? Well, I just knew.

When my time came, I drove to the hospital and told them the baby was coming. The nurses didn't believe me! They said it was too short a labor for a first baby. I lost my temper and yelled for the nurses to look at me as I was sure the birth was happening soon. They did and it was. They quickly rolled me into the delivery room, called the absent doctor, then urged me not to push. Not push? Try holding the water back when the dam bursts! My doctor entered the delivery room just in time to catch my Aries son who popped out like a champagne cork! As I wasn't sedated, there was no need to turn him upside down and whack his bottom. The fashion had changed and it so happened I was the only expectant mother in the hospital to opt for a natural childbirth. After our son was born, people kept dropping by to ask if I really had had a totally natural childbirth. I would respond, "What do you think our grandparents did?"

Back in my room, I called Skidmore College where Raja was lecturing in upstate New York. Surrounded by young women, he was embarrassed when I told him that he had a son. His response was "Hmmm." The next day, he returned to Texas and I left the hospital for our newly acquired home.

My family relented, reinstating me, and doted on their first grandchild and first great-grandchild. Mother came and stayed for three days to help with the baby. Love had triumphed after all. And now, I was a mother at twenty-one. Life is unexpected and sometimes a complete and wonderful mystery.

The early years with my son, Christopher, were magical. Never having had siblings, it was all new to me and every day a learning. In the hospital just after his birth, I tried to recall what I had read about nursing a baby. (I had ordered two books from Foyles in London and had them posted to me in France when I found out I was pregnant. One on what happens during the nine months in the womb and the other, Dr. Spock, on what to do with a newborn.) For instance, how to begin nursing? As I was pondering this in my hospital room, my young son, just born, reached up and grabbed my breast with his hungry mouth! I realized then and there that he would be my best teacher. I am sure it is largely biological but he became my world and it was a world of continuous joy and discovery for many years.

Our first Christmas was great fun. Raja, born a Hindu, of course never celebrated Christmas. I found a large piece of driftwood while hiking. Painting it white, I nailed it to a square piece of wood so that it would stand upright. Then I hung gum drops, candy canes, and tiny elves on the branches. Christopher was delighted. Raja and I — baby in the stroller — would daily walk to campus which was only a few blocks from our flat. As always, we never tired of long dialogues.

Once Timothy Leary came to Austin to meet with Raja. Leary was a psychologist from Harvard who hailed LSD as a philosophy of mind expansion and personal truth. After leaving Harvard, he continued to publicly promote the use of psyche-delic drugs and became a well-known cult figure of the counterculture. He coined the phrase "turn on, tune in, drop out." Fired from Harvard, Leary was later arrested due to his involvement with LSD. Soon to face trial, he thought Raja Rao might testify in his favor. After a lengthy discussion in our living room, Raja politely refused to testify on his behalf, not being in favor of drugs.

Another time, Nobel Prize-winning chemist Ilya Prigogine (known for his work in irreversible thermodynamics) came to speak philosophy with my husband. We also invited John Silber, who was a devotee of philosopher, Emanuel Kant. Though the flat was rather small to entertain, Raja suggested that I simply throw a white bedsheet on the living room floor, and we could sit on the floor and eat there. Raja directed the scientist to study Samkhya Philosophy. Samkhya philosophy regards the universe as consisting of two realities, purusha (consciousness) and prakriti (matter). The word Samkhya means reason, calculate. It is thought to be pre-Hindu so more than five thousand years old. The scientists were amazed to discover that many of the modern discoveries in physics were already recorded in these ancient Sanskrit texts. In my early twenties, my world was ever-expanding. For instance, I came to appreciate that like J. Robert Oppenheimer, one of the fathers of the A-Bomb, who recited from the *Bhagavad Gita*:

"Now I am become Death, the destroyer of worlds." Often these scientists are also spiritual seekers.

I have many good memories of intense and fascinating discussions, and also of our five-year-old son playing chess with a Nobel scientist. I had taught him to play chess and later table tennis. My system was simple. I never played down to him but always played to win. Then when I was too far ahead, I would simply turn the board around and again play to win. By the age of five, Christopher would champion me at chess and several years later, also at table tennis.

There were however some darker memories as well from the turbulent sixties. Drugs were part of the 1960s and Austin was no exception. Sometimes those same seekers would turn to drugs in their questing journey. Charles Gandy was one of these. Charles was a former Rhodes Scholar — I had actually had a date with him before I met my husband. After one date, I found him a bit too intense and did not see him again until after my marriage to Raja. Charles, though brilliant, had taken scores of LSD trips and though now more than somewhat mad, had amassed a devoted following. Charles felt it his mission to rescue my son and me from Raja Rao, whom he considered the anti-Christ. He began to camp outside our door. I drove to Dallas with Christopher, asking my mother and grandparents to keep our son until the situation was safe, then quickly returned to Austin, three and a half hours away.

Charles Gandy persisted in his nightly vigils. Once Raja said to invite him in. He ate little and lived on Hoffman's protein pills. Charles was tall and very, very strong. Once to demonstrate his strength, he lifted with one hand the heaviest chair in our living room and held it high over his head! After that, we did not let him inside the house. After several nights of standing guardian at our gate and sending written threats, we called the police. Charles had a full-blown breakdown and was committed to the State mental hospital. Somehow, he escaped and mysteriously disappeared for several months. Later we heard that he and his followers — mostly women — were staying in a wood on the outskirts of town when he disappeared. Almost a year later, we learned that he had died in that wood and that animals had torn him up, scattering his body parts over a two-mile radius in the forest. They knew this because they found his teeth and traced the dental records! What a sad waste of a once brilliant mind.

Then there was Mort Windisch, also a victim of too much LSD, who once followed us to New York. But Mort, though unbalanced, was no danger — except to himself. I heard that not long afterwards, he ended his own life by hanging.

One positive development was that my former mentor, the Shakespearean director B. Iden Payne and my husband became friends. And the four of us, husbands and wives, would take short holidays together — for instance, driving to San Antonio and staying the weekend at the famed Menger Hotel (1905) where O. Henry, Oscar Wilde, and Carrie Nation had been guests, and where Col. Theodore Roosevelt from the

Menger Bar, recruited his "Rough Riders". Other Presidents who stayed at the Menger Hotel included Ulysses S. Grant, Woodrow Wilson, and Dwight Eisenhower. Mr. Payne, a spiritual seeker, had always longed to go to India yet the Theatre and Shakespeare had claimed him as their own. Once driving home late evening from San Antonia to Austin, I looked out at all the lights from homes of those I had never met, and said aloud, "I always wonder about all the people I will never meet." And Mr. Payne said, "I've always wondered that, too." I was gratified that a few years later, I would help to find a publisher for Mr. Payne's autobiography, *Inside the Wooden O* (Yale University Press), the title a reference to Shakespeare's Globe Theatre in seventeenth century London. Though Mr. Payne never went to India, India came to him in the early seventies when my Teacher visited from India.

During the first three years of our marriage, I was content to be wife and mother. I had decided not to pursue the acting career professionally until my son was five as I believed Freud's findings that these formative years are vital in a child's life. Of course, by now I knew that Raja Rao could never be a traditional husband or father. His priority was clear: his writing. Mine at this time was Raja and Christopher, husband and son. I even slowly learned to cook a few vegetarian dishes. When I married, I had never cooked anything. However, once we settled in

Austin, I began to learn. We had a lot of pasta that first year! Raja taught me some simple Indian dishes. Being vegetarian was no problem as I had leaned in that direction for years due to my love for animals. We raised our son to be vegetarian as well. Twenty years later, I began to eat fish and poultry which came as a great shock to my son! I became aware that my blood type was Type O, the same as the Neanderthals. This blood type requires more protein than other types such as A or B. For years when I had to travel, living in hotels, with acting and play-writing, I lived on baked potato, green salad, and grilled cheese sandwiches! Unlike today, there were few menu selections for strict vegetarians. I was young then and fortunately youth over-comes many challenges.

Restless, I began to act in local plays in Austin. Acting locally and receiving rave reviews, I soon became a big fish in a small pond. I knew that I must either quit acting or go to New York, the mecca for serious theatre. When the time came, Raja was supportive in my decision to go to New York in order to try my wings. Raja's best friend, Bert, the owner of the African diamond mines, had forbidden his wife, a talented singer, to work in show business and both she and their marriage had suffered because of it. Wisely, my husband said I must go to New York. Somehow, we would manage both the marriage and the care of our young son, now almost two. So, we decided to spend the upcoming summer months in New York City and in nearby Poughkeepsie where Bert had a second home, an early nineteenth century farm house, which stood empty. As my husband could not finance my dream — he had little revenue working only half-time at the university — for the first time I had to support myself.

Summer came and with it, a new life began. One week after arriving in New York, I auditioned and was accepted to study with Lee Strasberg, founder of the Actors Studio. It was a rule that if accepted into Lee's private class, actors could not accept job offers as 'the work' with Strasberg was more important. The work was intensely emotional where you were called upon to dig deep and use your own past in such exercises as 'sense memory' and 'emotional recall' I was twenty-two and Strasberg terrified me as I felt his mode of teaching could be destructive. (Marilyn Monroe, James Dean, and Montgomery Cliff all worked with Lee, and, with other underlying tendencies, all ended their lives too early.)

As I had to earn a living, after a few weeks, I accepted a job and left the coveted class. My first acting job was in *The Happy Haven* by John Arden. It starred a known Broadway character actor, Lou Gilbert, who had recently acted in *8 ½*, Fellini's amazing film, now a cult classic.

Weekends proved idyllic in upstate New York in Bert's

large nineteenth century farm house with several hundred surrounding acres. The European couple who worked for Bert, stayed on to care for us. I would drive to Poughkeepsie each week for two days to spend as much time as possible with my young son and husband. Christopher spent considerable time looking at the cows and one morning said his first word, 'cow'. My husband, born a Hindu, was very pleased as the cow is considered sacred in India.

I auditioned for a new musical called *Hair* — also soon to be a Broadway hit. I knew only one song, *The Water is Wide,* a song I had sung in Austin in three productions of *Spoon River* (adapted from Edgar Lee Masters poems). The director and producers liked it, and called me back requesting a second song. The problem was I had no second song and knew that I was not a trained singer. It's important to know what you can't do.

Soon after, I auditioned for a new play which had been a recent hit in London. After a grilling two weeks of auditions beginning with over two thousand applicants for this one role, I was cast as Ophelia in Tom Stoppard's *Rosencrantz and Guildenstern*, which became the hit of the Broadway season. Torn between going to India in search of Truth and following a career in the theatre, I had vowed that if I won the Broadway role, I would stay and pursue acting. If not, I would go to India with my husband and pursue the spiritual. Then fate intervened. Two days after I was given the part, I was told that they had decided to bring the actor who had played Hamlet in the West End production in London to New York — unfortunately, he was six inches shorter than I was. I was offered instead to understudy the role of Ophelia and to play a walk-on part as her lady-in-waiting. Honoring my vow, I said no and opted to go with my husband and son to India.

After two years living in India, we began a commuting marriage (Austin and New York) long before it became a fashion and I was able to support myself doing what I loved: acting. Summers were spent together, one month at Christmas, and weekends and holidays whenever possible. Our marriage became a marriage of correspondence. Raja, ever a magnet with women, responded in kind. Though love was still there, I grew to understand that sometimes love is not enough.

The summer of 1973 found us all in Washington DC. Raja was chosen to be a Woodrow Wilson Institute Scholar for one year. His office was in the Smithsonian Institute. Christopher was seven and it was a magical time for him to discover the Smithsonian treasures, and other historical monuments of our country. It was also the year of the Watergate Scandal and the end of Richard Nixon's reign in the White House. Wherever we went, the topic was Watergate. We became friends with a radio journalist for NPR so kept abreast with what was happening. And, like many, became glued to the television watching the Watergate investigations and interviews with those Nixon supporters who were soon to be indicted and jailed.

One evening, the NPR radio journalist and a woman who worked in the White House came to dinner. Our son listened to all the disparaging remarks about our President and said he felt sorry for Nixon. The woman who worked in the White House said, "Well, if you really feel that way, why not write to him and tell him. I'm sure he would appreciate it." Well, this seven-year-old got up from the table and went to his room, returning several minutes later with a letter addressed to President Nixon. About two weeks later, a letter addressed to Christopher Rao came from The White House! My mother — who had voted for Nixon — was very pleased that he had personally replied to her grandson:

THE WHITE HOUSE

July 11, 1973

Dear Christopher,

No matter how busy the day is, I always enjoy hearing from young friends.

I am glad to see you are interested in the world around you. There is much joy and opportunity of life in America — if we only take the time to find it. Keep up the good work!

With my best wishes to you for the years ahead,

Richard Nixon

Rajeshwar Dayal, former Ambassador to Paris and later Foreign Secretary for Indira Gandhi, and his wife were also in Washington at this time. Rajeshwar, too, was a fellow of the Woodrow Institute, so we saw quite a lot of each other. John Owen, for thirty years the head of Serengeti National Park in Africa was another fellow scholar. John was a lovely English gentleman and became a dear friend of all of us. He was sad though, missing Africa, his home for three decades, "I miss my lions," he would say.

Before I left NY for the summer, I had been cast to play Gandhi's wife in a new play, *Gandhi*, directed by the well-known director, Jose Quintero. I had the script with me and studied it while in Washington. As I was about to return to begin rehearsals end of the summer, the director, Jose Quintero, informed me that I would not be in the play. The playwright had insisted that a friend of his be cast in the role of Kasturba. That's show biz.

Returning to NY, I soon found other work. Raja returned to Austin to teach. And life moved on. The marriage, however, suffered due to absences. My husband soon found other women — younger women — to comfort him. Being psychic, I would always know when he was with someone else — even with thousands of miles between us. And when I returned home to

Austin, I would pick up on the energies of another woman having been in the rooms. Raja never denied it. When the current liaison became pregnant, Raja would urge her to have an abortion. Later when he became involved with a friend of mine, she was determined to have the child. He made it clear that it would not be his responsibility. She never married but raised their son on her own. There is often a shadow side with great men.

> Ever has it been that love knows not its own depth
> until the hour of separation.
>
> Khalil Gibran

The hardest part was leaving our son, Christopher, with my mother and step-father, Harry — for a time while I could stabilize my career and earn enough to bring him to New York. So, from the second grade, his beginning school years were spent in Texas with many visits back and forth. At this time, most of the acting work I was cast in was playing leading roles out of town, regional theatres like in Cincinnati or Florida. Most nights I would call my son and sing him to sleep. It was hard but I knew that if I suppressed the passion for acting, I would not be a good mother.

When Christopher turned eleven, after living with my mother and stepfather for four years, he came to NY where he would stay with me until he left for university. I could no longer bear the separation, and fortunately, he felt the same.

Raja continued to live in Austin, teaching and writing his novels. The good thing was that though there were 'spaces in our togetherness' as Khalil Gibran once wrote of marriage, the times we came together as a family were special. I did not ask for any financial assistance and supplemented my theatre income with teaching, initially substitute teaching in high schools and later teaching graduate playwriting at The New School University. Also, in the seventies and eighties, one could live much less expensively than today in NY. So, for a while, this commuting marriage seemed to work for all concerned.

Often our son and I would join Raja in Paris or India as well as visits in Austin. One year, Raja was invited to speak at a conference at the Sorbonne in Paris, and asked us to join him there. The cocktail reception was held at the President's Palace so we met President Mitterrand. There I met Peter Ustinov, actor and author, a very entertaining and bright mind. Bishop Tutu, the South African theologian and human rights activist in the anti-apartheid movement, clearly a man with a mission was there as well as the cultural critic, Susan Sontag, a colleague of mine at The New School. It was a varied group which always makes for a more stimulating gathering.

Christopher had hoped to meet Francis Ford Coppola,

the director of *The Godfather* films and many others. Somehow it didn't happen. To curb his disappointment, as we were leaving the President's Palace, I noticed a new computer store directly across the street. I suggested we go there as Christopher was fascinated by home computers which were still relatively new. As we entered the store, guess who was there? Yes, the one and only Francis Ford Coppola! Coppola and my son hit it off to such an extent that Coppola suggested we all have dinner together. So, we piled into a small Parisian taxi with Christopher sitting on Coppola's lap and drove to a nearby restaurant. Coppola had his own wine from his own vineyard that was lost on us as neither of us drank. But the conversation was lively and Coppola couldn't get over how Christopher reminded him of his precocious self at that age.

Back in NY, my son and I still had to live prudently. As all actors know, theatre work is intermittent. We were now living in Manhattan Towers, 37th floor, interspersed with time in India and Texas, often with Raja. Again, thanks to subsidized housing for performing artists and my son in a fine school, Hunter College High School, I could stop acting, stay put, and write. This meant I could be a mother for my son's next six or seven years in New York. No more out of town acting jobs. Life was good. And I was grateful.

We are mostly a family of two, plus Sebastian, our

wonderful feline. Sebastian, without being taught, had begun to use the toilet just as the other two human beings in the flat.

Christopher 12, Sebastian 5

There were perks in those days though. Daily in the basement of our building after 3 p.m., we could line up and purchase Broadway tickets for $1 each. My son and I saw the original cast in *Chorus Line* three times! Tickets were also available for opera, ballet, and concerts — providing the house was not sold out. As the British — now Broadway — hit, *Nicholas Nicholby* was sold out, we purchased two 'standing room' tickets for a hundred dollars. During the show, the cast intermingled with the audience and the leading actor, Roger Rees, surprised us by coming up to Christopher and talking to him for some time. The show was long covering both a matinee and later a full evening performance for Part 2. So, along with two actor friends, John and Jillian, we went out for a sit-down dinner near the Broadway theatre. One could also have free entrance to all the great museums on one day each week, which we did. Once a week, my son and I would go out for dinner, usually at *Curtain Up* downstairs. The rule was apart from the entre you could order either a drink or dessert but not both. Christopher thought it was a game and enjoyed deciding each week which one he would order. Years later, he commented, "Mother, I didn't realize we were poor when we lived in New York." That touched me.

After acting in over fifty-five productions both in and out of New York, I began to write plays. (See New York Part IV) Oddly, I did not miss the acting and viewed those years as a preparation to the writing of plays — and later screenplays. Once in an interview, I was asked if I missed acting. I replied, "No, not really. The difference is that now I play all the roles!"

The strongest principle of growth
lies in human choice.

George Eliot

During my son's senior year, another unexpected experience emerged. I met a charming Frenchman in New York and fell in love with a man my own age. Let's call him Charles. It sounds like a Woody Allen film but Charles and I met while standing in line for an exhibition at the Museum of Modern Art. It was a passionate union from the start. Charles though French had been educated in England: Sandhurst, Oxford, then Harvard in the States for his doctorate in film. His ambition was to write novels and films. Apart from his boyish good looks, he talked like Masterpiece Theatre, that sexy upper-class Oxfordian English. I was smitten. We grew close over a year and a half and I joined him in a trip to London to meet his family. His father had been knighted due to his business prowess, and I got along well with all his family. Charles proposed and his family was grateful to see that their son was settling down.

About the time my play, *Calamity Jane* received its first of many productions, I was notified that I was chosen for a Fulbright Research grant in India, I took Christopher out of school with the understanding that he had to do his school work and keep a journal of the trip. Charles planned to visit me in India. (Part III: India)

Returning to New York, it was time for Christopher to go to university. He was given a full scholarship to University of Texas-Austin, my alma-mater and where his father still taught philosophy. After he went off to college, with his permission, I invited Charles to move into Manhattan Plaza and give up his apartment downtown. Now formally engaged, we lived together for a time — which, of course, is when you really get to know someone. Charles was charming but grew unreasonably possessive. He became jealous even of my women friends. Perhaps I was too bound to freedom at this point. Also, though we were the same age, Charles seemed immature and even occasionally unstable — almost violent.

I was invited to Yaddo, a respected art colony, in upstate New York. Charles was worried that the separation might harm our relationship so he visited and stayed at a local B&B. I spent the day writing and would join him in the evenings during his visit before his return to New York City, to what was now 'our' apartment.

During one of my earlier four stays at Yaddo, I had met the remarkable artist and author, Anne Truitt (1921-2004) and we had become fast friends. When I told her about Charles and that he wanted to marry, she said she wanted to meet him, to check him out. She came up from Washington DC and we had lunch at her club. After lunch, she invited Charles to join us for coffee and dessert, then to leave. After he left, she turned to me and said, "Catherine, I don't know what to say. He's not yet formed." I understood at once what she meant though I didn't end the relationship. At least, not then.

Since Charles wanted us to marry, he was keen that I get

a divorce. When Christopher turned eighteen, I asked for a divorce. Raja did not want to divorce as our marriage had now become a convenient shield. In other words, he could have his women and yet not be available to fully commit. Of course, this had been true for some time. At last, my husband reluctantly agreed. Our marriage had lasted twenty years, giving us a remarkable son, and though ever a challenge, as I told Raja when I finally asked for the divorce, "I was never bored." He liked that.

There was no contention. It was time and the divorce went through quickly. I asked for nothing — not even for our son. I even paid for the divorce and won my freedom. I remember Raja saying to me, "Don't ask. Never ask anything. Find your dharma ('law of your existence'— much more than career). Live for work. Don't work to live. Allow your madness totally." Strange how you can admire a man who caused such suffering.

Meanwhile Charles had asked me to stop focusing on my career and instead support his goal as a writer. At this point, I had written several plays that were produced in and out of New York and won awards while Charles was writing his first novel. Still very much infatuated, I agreed knowing I did not have to talk about a writing career but could simply quietly write. Yet later I pondered, "If someone truly loves you, would they ask such a thing?" In the end, I decided not to marry again, so after a year and a half, with Christopher now at the university in Texas, my French lover left. Empty nest.

Though I had my work writing plays and also teaching writing at The New School, I was surprised how acutely I felt the 'empty nest' as Christopher and I were quite close. I had tried to raise him as an independent spirit so it was only natural that he flew away.

As Fate would have it, after the Fulbright Research grant in India, in 1985-1986, I was invited to be a guest professor the following year at The University of Texas in Austin, where my son would be a sophomore. Christopher surprised me by suggesting we be roommates! "You don't want to be roommates with your mother when you're at college!" He responded, "Yes, I do. It will be fun." So, against my better judgment but to my delight, we discovered that the duplex in front of our former garage apartment was free. Raja had married his current girlfriend, a trained nurse two years younger than myself. And they had moved across town.

So, we rented one half of the duplex. A 2-BR, 2 BATH, kitchen, living room and dining room with both up and down stairs. And a short walk to campus. I had told my son that, "Being roommates or housemates means sharing cleaning, shopping, cooking." That shows how naïve I was! Still it was fun and our schedules were so busy that we often passed in the night.

Christopher, College Man

During one of our annual visits to India, my son and I saw a remarkable thing — two cobras mating near our Teacher's Home in Kerala. I wrote it up and it was later published when asked for a personal essay on *marriage* in an anthology with that theme.

How Two Cobras Changed My Life

Several years ago, I was living with my young son in a small village in south India pursuing spiritual studies. Earlier in Paris, I had wed a brilliant man from south India and was now, some years later considering a divorce. I stand near a sacred river in Kerala, where it is said the god Rama sailed to Ceylon (Sri Lanka) to rescue his wife, Sita from the ten-headed demon, Ravana.

Immersed in the humidity and sensuality of tropical India, which is itself a living dream, it seemed almost natural when two five-foot long cobras slowly approached each other. Standing about six feet away, I watch them for over an hour dancing the ancient dance of the mating game. Their tails intertwine while the upper bodies, facing each other, sway to the hidden music of Eastern erotica. It is no less than the cosmic dance of Shiva, enticing and sublime.

Two village girls excitedly and fearfully gestured that I should come away quickly and go inside the house. I listened as they told me this story. In typical India fashion, I will now relate a story within a story. Five years before in nearby Aranmula, a five-year-old boy was playing near the ancient Aranmula Temple and came upon two cobras mating. The little boy threw stones at them and suddenly the male copra reared his head and stared straight at the boy in a piercing manner. The cobras returned to their business while the boy ran away and thought little of it afterwards. However, late that same evening, as the little village boy lay in a one room hut with his family, all sleeping in the same room, that same male cobra found the boy, bit him, and killed him. Understandably, I was strongly urged to not disturb these cobras and to keep my distance. I returned to the scene though not so close now and stood quietly lest I disturb them.

Mesmerized, the time flew. Later, after two hours of sexual delight, the two serpents shot upward in rocket orgasm, then — and here's the amazing part — slowly uncoiled, slithering away in opposite directions!

The answer was clear: what is sublime and true may reach its purpose, and afterward those, once bound, may — as in nature —unbind and go their separate paths. Let each moment be sufficient unto itself. And when over, allow the simple act of going one's own separate way, without judgment or regret. Such is the memory of marriage, where sex and bliss, positive and negative residues reside, giving birth to a new life.

Though they will never know how they changed my life, I will forever be grateful to those two wonderful cobras! And, my experience has taught me that divorce need not mean that the marriage was a failure, only that it is time to go our separate ways, as did those two amazing cobras in India.

1986: After the divorce, this telegram arrived from India:

> Arrived here Wednesday. Your Letter
> brought happiness. Wish you and
> Christopher a year of pure fulfillment!
>
> Raja

Christopher, New Mexico

After my son's graduation, he was admitted to Harvard Law School and the Kennedy School working on joint degrees during his four years there. For one year he also studied Chinese medicine. Fortunately, by that time, I was working in Hollywood so could afford to cover most of his ivy league education. He graduated with cum laude honors and moved to Seattle, Washington where he met the lovely Josie, married, and after a few years, had two sons, Raja and Tristan — my grandsons. Christopher opened his own law office near their home, and became a fine husband and father as well.

Christopher visited his father in 2005 to introduce him to his first grandson and namesake, Raja, born August 2005, but sadly my son later told me that Raja didn't recognize his son or grandson due to advanced dementia. A year later, Raja Rao died of heart failure, July 8, 2006, at his home in Austin, Texas, at the age of ninety-seven.

I remembered years before when someone asked Raja about death, he replied, "Death, for me, is simply going from one room into another."

- Raja Rao, philosopher & novelist, nominated for the Nobel Prize in Literature.
- 1964: 1964: Sahitya Akademi Award
- 1969: Padma Bhushan
- 1970s: Indian of the Year Award
- 1987: Neustadt International Prize for Literature
- 2007: Padma Vibhushan

Raja, though perhaps not necessarily the best husband and father material, was a great author and most certainly a unique individual. There could never be one like him. I shall always be grateful to him, both for our son and for introducing us to the Sage. Here is a revealing quote from one of his later novels, *The Chessmaster and His Moves:*

> My mind was essentially metaphysical …
>> thus evading the human.
> For, after all, the human has no ultimate significance.

Raja Rao (1908-2006)

⯑

Part III Awakening: India

How do I know about the world?

By what is within me.

Lao Tzu

In New York City, after I was removed as a 'too tall' Ophelia in the Broadway production of Tom Stoppard's *Rosencrantz and Guildenstern* and turned down the offer of lady-in-waiting plus understudying Ophelia, the role I had originally been cast in, I prepared to pursue a long-time wish to travel to India in search of a spiritual teacher. With Raja and our young son, Christopher, I would embrace my husband's land, India, which would prove a catalyst for deep, inner change. I left for a month and remained in India for the next two years.

Almost at once, upon our arrival, I knew I had come home. On our first day there, I wrote:

> India is home. Nothing surprises.
> I have been here before.
>
> Journal, 1968

Raja's Spiritual Search:
After Raja Rao wrote his first novel in his early twenties, *Kanthapura* — considered now a classic in India and elsewhere — he stopped writing and began a ten-year search for a spiritual master or guru. He lived for a year with Nobel Prize author Rabindranath Tagore in Calcutta, Bengal.

Rabindranath Tagore (1861 – 1941)

He then travelled to the Himalayan mountains in N. India and studied with a Yogi Sadhu (one who has renounced the world) who lived in a cave. Then he was invited by Gandhi to live in his ashram for one year to translate letters from French to English.

Mahatma Gandhi (1869-1948)

Next, he travelled to S. India to Pondicherry, near Madras, and for one year, stayed at the ashram of Sri Aurobindo and his consort, Mother, who was a French woman. Then not far away, also near Madras, he met the great sage who inspired Somerset Maugham to write *The Razor's Edge*, Sri Ramana Maharshi, who was still living. After another year spent there, questioning and searching, it was Ramana Maharshi himself who directed Raja to go to Kerala and meet the Householder Sage.

Finally, after searching for ten long years, Raja's quest ended among the towering, tropical palm trees of Kerala and wide, sacred rivers. His second and most autobiographical novel, *The Serpent and the Rope*, is about his search for Truth, ending with finding the Guru. Finding the right spiritual teacher is like finding the right partner multiplied by a thousand. You simply know beyond doubt and your life is forever transformed.

Now, years later, my husband wanted to go to Kerala where his Guru's ashes were interned in a private ashram. Being of an independent nature, I told him that I wished to search for my own teacher and not simply follow his path. Raja agreed, cleverly suggesting only that first we travel to the ashram in Kerala, in south India. Christopher, almost two, was a born traveler, which made the long trip easier.

Our first stop was Bombay (now Mumbai) where we stayed for two nights at the amazing Taj Mahal Hotel, which stands upon the shore at the Gateway to India initially built to welcome Queen Victoria, who never came to India. We were invited for tea in the Malabar Hills by a friend of Raja's, Meera Sarabhai, the daughter of a wealthy industrialist and patron of the arts. At tea, she asked me if I had heard of the philosopher J. Krishnamurti. I replied that I had read two of his books when I was nineteen. She asked if I would like to meet him as he was currently her house guest. I said yes and was shown into a large guest bedroom while Raja waited in the living room with Meera and our son.

J. Krishnamurti

A moment later, Krishnamurti, dressed in white Indian clothes, emerged through a terrace door, long white curtains billowing softly from an ocean breeze. He was strikingly handsome and very intense. We sat on his bed and talked for well over an hour. I told K that I came to India to find a spiritual teacher, a Guru. This upset him and he asked why a Guru? I replied that even Adi Shankar, the great Vedantic Sage of the 8th century had said, "I am the Absolute through the words of my Guru." Then K took me by both shoulders and vigorously shook me, saying, "Shankara is dead ashes!"

Another time I told him that since early childhood I had felt that what is real is within me and what is without is not real. Again, he became impatient and suddenly stood up, grabbing my hand and pulling me to the open terrace door. K pointed below to some street children and said, "Look at those poor beggars. How can you tell me they are not real?" I withdrew my hand and simply said, "I can only say that what is within is more real than what is perceived outside." I saw his look of impatient disappointment and frustration. Not long afterwards, with my husband and son, I left the house.

Later I realized that this 'chance' meeting was necessary to erase the imprint I had from reading K's transcribed talks, and be open to meeting the Sage.

From the age of seven I had experienced a recurrent dream, simple yet very powerful. In the dream, I am in the backseat of a car that is being driven, although there is no visible driver in the front seat. The car drives into a heated desert, suddenly stopping as the back, right door swings open by itself. I look up and see above me a large rock and from behind the rock, a striking dark-skinned man appears wrapped in a white cloth around his waist and a white shirt. At this moment, I have the distinct feeling that I have come Home. I dreamt this again and again over the years until I was twenty-three and arrived in India.

Kerala, India

Two days after the meeting with J. Krishnamurti, we flew from Bombay to Cochin, a seaport in Kerala. After spending the night at the Malabar Hotel, we took a taxi and drove for three hours until we slowed almost to a stop as a large female elephant and her young one turned off the main road into a narrow dirt road leading to a small village where the secluded ashram was located. Raja was very happy, saying the elephants were a very auspicious sign. So, we respectfully, if slowly, followed in the taxi behind the graceful lumbering, ever patient elephants. Here was another mother and child going to the ashram for the first time.

Arriving at the entrance to the ashram below a spreading, ancient mango tree, the taxi stopped. Someone opened the backseat door and I looked up and saw a striking dark-skinned man, dressed in white dhoti and white Western shirt, emerge from the front door of a white stone home with a sloping, red-tiled roof. Yes, this was the same figure from the recurrent dream I had experienced since age seven. And, as in the dream, there was the distinct feeling that I had come Home.

Words mean nothing and prove only
interruptions to Experience.

Journal, Feb 1968

As it happened, I was the only Westerner staying in the village which aroused much curiosity among the local natives. The children would encircle me, calling out, "What is your name? What is your name?" possibly the only English they knew. When I repeated the question to them, they would laugh and laugh then run away.

After two or three weeks of daily enjoying the presence

of the Sage (also a Householder Sage as was His Father), my husband left to meet some people who had optioned his novel, *The Serpent and the Rope*, for a Hollywood film. I opted to remain with the Sage and His Family. Only a few days later, Raja cabled, requesting me to join him in Bangalore. As I took leave of Sri Gurudev and His Family, He said, "You had wanted to meet other spiritual people so now perhaps you will. I smiled and shook my head 'no' saying, "That was before I came here." He added that there were other teachers and ashrams such as Sai Baba, Ramana Maharshi, Ananda Mayi, Aurobindo, and Mahesh Yogi. I laughed and said, "No, no, please. I have already found what I sought."

> The world is a reality
> Only to itself,
> Not to Me.

Journal, 1968

Reluctantly, I flew to Bangalore with Christopher, arriving a day before Raja who was meeting the Hollywood men in Delhi. We were all to be guests of Dr. Gokak, the Vice-Chancellor of Bangalore University. There was an older couple, already guests of Dr. Gokak. The Osbornes, originally from England and Poland, had lived many years in Tiruvannamalai, Tamil Nadu, near Madras (now Chennai) with Ramana Maharshi.

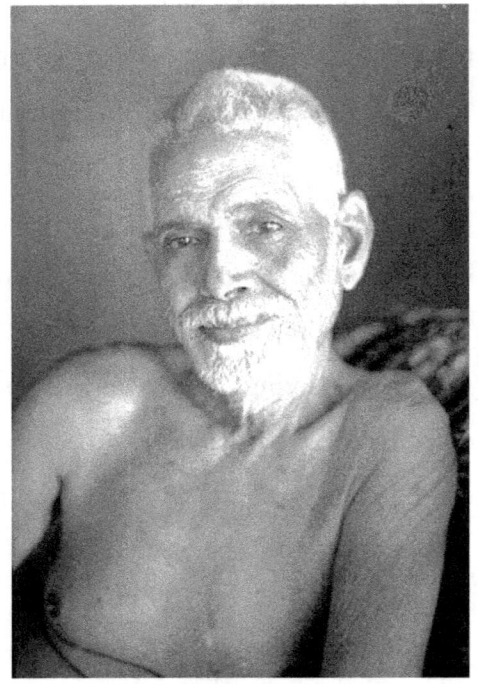

Sri Ramana Maharshi (1879 – 1950)

In fact, this Englishman and his Polish wife, were the first to record, translate, and publish the sayings of Ramana into English, beginning with *Who Am I?* I noticed books of Ramana all over the house as well as those of Aurobindo, a sage and poet who, had passed away the same year as Ramana, 1950.

Dr. Gokak shared with us that he had been for many years a follower of Sri Aurobindo, but that now, he was a devotee of Sai Baba who lived here near Bangalore.

An eerie feeling came over me as I recalled the parting words of Sri Gurudev only a few hours before! He had

122

mentioned all three of these Indian teachers to me as I was taking leave.

Sathya Sai Baba (1926-2011)

Later that day, Gokak came excitedly to tell me that there was to be a private dinner with Sai Baba this evening, and he had received permission to bring me along. I went and as several people were prostrating on the floor to Sai Baba, I simply stood and respectively bowed with a namaste, with folded hands.

The next day Raja arrived along with Arnold Schulman, the screenwriter, Claude Giroux, the French-Canadian producer, and Claude's wife, Maureen. Schulman had already heard of Sai Baba and was eager to meet him so Gokak who was also head of the Sai Baba Foundation, arranged for a private audience for

Sri Aurobindo (1872-1950)

all of us to attend the following day. After arriving at the
expansive ashram, we waded through hundreds of people who
were patiently waiting for Sai Baba to appear. Ushered into the
house to an empty room, we had only just arrived when Sai Baba
entered and bade us sit on the floor, as did he. Baba spoke simply
as Gokak translated. "Be good to one another" and "I give them
what they want (the material things) so that they will later want
what I want." It all seemed rather simplistic — even cliché —
after having been with the Kerala Sage for three weeks. Young
Christopher ran about. When Baba created sacred ash or busman
from the air, he gave a handful to our son, at which point,
Christopher went around the circle and put ash on each forehead,

sharing his treasure. When he came to Sai Baba, Baba laughed and would not allow him to bless him with the ash. Instead, he gently turned Christopher around and placed him squarely on his lap, still laughing.

Maureen, Giroux's wife, had been having severe stomach pains and feared it was her appendix as a doctor had already diagnosed. Baba reached high into the air and magically created more busman or ashes and gave it to her, saying to place half in a glass of water today and the other half tomorrow morning. She did so and the pain went away, never to return.

Sai Baba's final action was to create a gold and ruby ring from the air with a twirl of his hand then present it to Raja. We left Sai Baba as it was time for him to greet the waiting multitude outside. A few minutes later, we stood near two long lines of expectant devotees as Sai Baba walked between the endless lines of people, occasionally pausing to place his hand upon their heads. I wondered if this was something like the time of Jesus when he healed the multitudes. Though he might not be the highest level, one could see that he possessed certain siddhis or powers. Later Schulman insisted each of us try on the unasked gift bestowed upon my husband, and amazingly the gold and ruby ring would not fit any of us — only Raja who had very slim fingers. (A few months later Schulman returned to India and spent several months with Sai Baba in order to write the first biography about the charismatic yogi.) And when Raja returned to Kerala, he threw the ring into the holy river near the private ashram. Why? I suppose a gesture to the true Sage who lived here.

The next day we all flew north to Benares (Varanasi), an ancient and amazing city where Hindus wish to die or at least have their ashes scattered on the Sacred Ganga.

Benares. A universe, layers behind layers confusedly blended into One. Contradictions abounded: the smell of incense and urine; sadhus and cow dung; pigeons and vultures; the mythic purity of the Sacred Ganga River and the corruption where street beggars mutilate their own children — blinding them or cutting off a hand — to increase their revenue from begging. Here were not beautiful faces as expected but rather ones of holy resignation, a surrender to their individual and collective fate. Even the sacred cows seem evolved souls as I perceived past ages of India in their accepting eyes. Unchanged for centuries, ancient India was strong in the air.

At dusk, we were in a small boat passing the holy Ghats where nightly bodies are laid on stacks of wood and burned, a pyre to the afterlife. After the pyre is lit, the family sits in silence for three or more hours as ashes are returned to ashes. The sheer silence of the ritual was the poignant and overpowering aspect of it all. Suddenly an explosion! The boatman casually explained that someone forgot to crack the skull before lighting the flames in order to prevent the head exploding. This a final reminder of life's fragility. Then he pointed out a large, impressive house near the Ghats, "The largest house there is owned by the seller of firewood." Words failed to comprehend this often contradictory, holy city of Benares. It would take me years to absorb all that was experienced there. Only that to comprehend Benares is to understand the rich complexity that is India.

The purpose of this trip for the two Hollywood men was to scout locations as the film adaptation of Raja's novel, *The Serpent and the Rope*, would take place in Cambridge, Paris, Provence, south India, and Benares. We stayed at the Clark Hotel where it so happened Mahesh Yogi was staying with George Harrison, one of the Beatles. A BBC documentary film was being made of the rising popular yogi, soon to become known globally for *Transcendental Meditation*.

On the following day, we were walking in the streets of Banaras when Raja suddenly recognized that we were in front of the entrance to Ananda Mayi's Ashram. He said she may not be here as she has several ashrams and travels all the time. Raja rang the bell and she was there. As they knew Raja, we were ushered in to meet the frail but extraordinary Hindu saint.

Mostly in samadhi or transcendental states, Ananda Mayi is now fed by her devotees, otherwise she would forget to eat. She had the most wonderful smile and we felt blessed just to be in her glowing presence. She sweetly took my hand and smiled as she nodded. Happy to have seen her, I noted the difference between a saint as herself and a sage as my Guru. Though a saint may be realized, only a Sat Guru can enlighten others.

Ananda Mayi (1896-1982)

By now, I had unintentionally come in contact with all five of the spiritual teachers cited by my Guru! My aim was clear. I told Raja that I wished to return to Kerala without delay. He agreed, saying he would join me in a few days after the Hollywood people left. I took leave of the Hollywood folk, packed, meditated, and fell into a sound sleep. Soon I would be Home.

The next morning, with my son, I was boarding the plane when I saw a crowd surrounding Mahesh Yogi. The British director was standing off to the side and approached me, saying, "We began with a holy man and ended up with a prima donna!" He shared that daily Mahesh Yogi would keep the director and the entire crew waiting for hours in the torrid Indian sun while he performed his ritual bathing. Boarding the plane, it so happened that Mahesh Yogi was seated just across the aisle from my seat. First his Western attendant boarded and put a leopard skin on the seat and then the Yogi came and sat. Once in the air, I heard him speaking with his attendant.

Mahesh Yogi (1918-2008)

"That young woman looks serious. Ask her if she would like to ask me something."

The young man did and I politely declined, "Please thank him but tell him that I have already found my Guru." A moment later, I overheard the Mahesh Yogi complain about 'having to ride on public planes and shouldn't we have a private plane?'

Back home in Kerala, I hurriedly bathed in the river, left Christopher with our Indian ayar and walked to Sri Gurudev's House, finding Him sitting alone in what we called the Talk Room. After greeting, the words came tumbling out how in only a few days, I had met Sai Baba, Ananda Mayi, and Mahesh Yogi as well as disciples of Sri Aurobindo and Ramana Maharishi — the very ones you spoke of as I took leave! With a faint smile, He simply said, "Is it so?"

Content to be at home, in stillness, in sacred solitude.

A well-known astrologer came to the ashram and I learned that Sri Gurudev had studied astrology and would interpret when my chart was done, as the Malayali astrologer did not speak English. We three met in the little house next to the Family home. The astrologer was bald, in his sixties, and sat on the floor with a small wooden tray. He then emptied tiny, white sea shells which he moved around the wooden tray, using the shells to calculate instead of pencil and paper. He spoke of my past life in central India when I was a devotee of Krishna and had studied music and dance. He said that my husband died young of a broken heart when I left to stay with my guru whom I remained with until my death. My husband would return to search for me in this life and we would both continue the spiritual interest. He continued to say that when we were near, we would quarrel yet could not be apart. If apart, the husband would weep. That we quarrel because our love is so strong. Love is there. He spoke of my son who would be devoted and learned, and that mother and son would be very close. He said that my Venus, Sun, and Jupiter were all exalted, that is, at their zenith. That through my art, the spiritual would be seen. That I had been an actor for many lives and would continue in this life until the age of thirty-eight, after which I would focus on writing and teaching. (Actually, I would stop acting and seriously commit to writing at age thirty-three though I continued to do some acting for another few years.) He said that in a past life, I had been a yogini and misused some powers and this would manifest as brain problems in this life — which I understood to refer to my epilepsy. And that I would attain liberation. He also said that I would come and go to India until my death. I did not realize until years later how accurate all said would turn out to be.

The original plan was to spend one month in India. However, after the month was up and, having now met Sri Gurudev, when my husband returned to Austin to teach, I stayed on with Christopher for the next two years studying Advaita Vedanta, the philosophy behind Hinduism. Gratefully, my husband understood due to his own ten-year quest. There's a saying in India that "It's all right to be born in the temple as long as you don't die there." In other words, organized religion is a starting point to higher philosophy. In the Direct Approach through Advanta Vedanta, there is no concept or image of God — only Pure Consciousness. Though latent within, its experience must be awakened by a true sage. This was what I had longed for more than the theatre or even family life. I was in the right place at the right time. At twenty-three, I longed to know the Truth. After all, why else are we here?

I was born with a question mark in my soul.

Journal, 1968

The first or second night after meeting Sri Gurudev, another dream came. In the dream, Jesus Christ was sitting on a low wall under a tree, speaking to little children. This was the gentle Jesus I had sought, leaving one Texas church for another, seeking a more loving religion without fear or talk of damnation. In the dream, the Sage was passing by. Suddenly Jesus stood up, walked over to Sri Gurudev, and bowed with great respect. As I awoke, the meaning of the dream was crystal clear. For my own journey, Christianity had been a preparation so that now the

Christ within must bow to the Sage.

Years later, as a screenwriter in Hollywood, I learned the importance of the 'through-line' or, as I came to call it, 'the continuous thread'. What is the 'continuous thread' which links my life which I am now attempting to share? Gandhi cited his as the Search for Truth. Though a lesser subject, mine would hold this same principle. Gandhi changed history. The goal here was simply to change myself or rather to go to the end of that smaller self. Truth, if it be absolute, does not change. However, one's perception of it does, due to the capacity of perception which may evolve or diminish over time.

Who would think living in a third world village without glass windows or plumbing would be the most important and happiest years of my life? Christopher and I lived in a small cottage with two rooms, no bathroom or kitchen. We obtained our water by lowering a bucket into a nearby well. During the fierce monsoon rains, gathering a small child and an umbrella, and walking at night to the outhouse was a challenge. We bathed twice daily in the sacred river which was a ten minute walk each way, Christopher on my hip. Instead of glass, there were only bars on the windows so it was not uncommon to endure large mosquitoes, larger poisonous black spiders and over five-foot long serpents, including pythons and cobras. Once I came home to find a five-foot long, eight-inch wide chela (snake) under my bed! I called aloud for my servant, a teenage village girl, Uma, who entered and with a stick broom made from coconut palm, casually ushered the live iridescent yellow-green serpent outside — as though it was nothing at all!

March is the hottest month in Kerala and can reach 140 degrees Fahrenheit with 95% humidity as it is an extreme tropical climate. I had gone native and neglected to boil the well water, so, it was not surprising that I came down with amoebic dysentery, followed by severe dehydration. Unable to leave my bed due to weakness, I thought that this might be the end. It was then I saw the Sage on the subtle plane, standing at the foot of my bed. This was a premonition as a few minutes later, He arrived, now in the physical, in my room. I tried but was unable to stand due to weakness. Sri Gurudev said, "You have some physical difficulty. Otherwise, there's nothing wrong." I smiled. How incidental this slight malady of the body when I am There!

He instructed the servants to carry me in a chair to a waiting taxi and I was rushed to a nearby clinic in the nearest town, twenty minutes away. There the good Christian doctor injected glucose in both arms at once, saying that in another five minutes, it would have been the end of me. Two days later, I returned to my room at the ashram.

As I lay in illness, the half-opened windows carried to me the relentless beauty of tropical Kerala. Last night I heard the subtle groan of an aged banana leaf, slowly breaking from the hanging weight of itself and falling ever so gently to the ground. Who will care? Not even the tree itself.

Soon I would return to river bathing. What joy to immerse totally into the sacred river's gentle yet swift currents, as continuous as time. Then upon leaving the river, I spied flocks of clucking, bathing geese glide on the beach herded by their umbrella-carrying dark-skinned shepherd.

> All outward movement is a result of inner denial.
> We seek others from fear of knowing ourselves.
> Likewise, we fill up the air with chatter to drown
> the soaring sound of silence ever calling to us from
> within. Both saints and artists well know that it is
> solitude which feeds their strength. Beware of all
> things which attempt to steal away the solitary self.
>
> Journal, 1968

Sometimes an old Chinese master would stand to my left at the end of my bed, on the subtle plane, just before I went to sleep. I wasn't afraid. I felt he had been a teacher in a past life and was just making himself known to me. How many lives, how many teachers made it possible for me to meet the Sage in this life and to live here as part of His family. It is Grace. There is no other word.

135

When Christopher turned three, we were still living in the village in south India. No phones, no television, no plumbing. What toys he had we created from banana palm, coconut palm leaf, and other natural substances. However, I did manage to obtain paper and crayons from a nearby town twenty minutes away by auto rickshaw. One morning, I asked him to draw 'love' and without hesitation, he drew two wide blue circles. Young children do not have a sense of the right or wrong way to draw anything. They do not hesitate to draw a purple sky or red grass. They are not afraid to draw outside the lines. They create empty spaces to play. I consciously delayed teaching Christopher to read as I wished him to experience oneness with what he saw. That is, rather than see a 'tree' and knowing the label or word for it, he remained one with all he perceived.

Once I saw Christopher running along the shore of the river as about six young Malayali boys his age or older, squatted passively watching this energetic American! I shall always picture him on the sandy banks of the sacred river at sunset, calling, "Mommy! Mommy!" then running, crashing into my waiting arms. How happy he was there, himself a little villager.

When mango season arrived in April and May, I was invited to join the wife of Sri Gurudev and her two teenage daughters to hold a wide, white sheet while Prem, a tall, young servant shook the mango tree with a long pole. Suddenly, it was raining ripe mangos! Later I experienced the unforgettable taste of fresh mango and parboiled rice mixed with fresh yogurt, and eaten with one's own fingers off a daily picked green banana leaf in lieu of a plate. The rice was harvested from the family's own paddy and parboiled — so much healthier than ordinary bought rice. And the fresh yogurt came from their own cows.

I had little or no knowledge of how to be a disciple in this five-thousand-year-old Hindu tradition. Before India, for three years, I had ardently read the books of His Father who was also my husband's Guru. I meditated yet nothing seemed complete until I met the Sage. As the tradition says, as we are in the body, it is necessary to meet a living, realized soul or Teacher in order for that 'inner guru' which is in us to be awakened. Now, being in the presence of a living sage, I understood my earlier failure to be satisfied in spite of my solitary efforts. A living teacher is essential.

My husband's Guru — already a great soul — met his Guru only once in physical form, but this was sufficient. In the years to follow, though they continued to meet on the subtle level, they would never again meet in the physical. The Guru chooses the one to carry on, and his spiritual energies are transferred to this one disciple.

Wife of Sri Gurudev

Though Sri Gurudev never asked to be the one, he was chosen by his father and Guru so could not refuse. Even so, after His Guru's passing, Sri Gurudev withdrew to the small village where His mother and father's ashes were interred and lived a solitary life, with his wife and three children. In spite of this, after some years, both Indian and Western seekers found their way to his door, and his spiritual dharma began.

No true Guru will say that he is the one. Once an older American woman came to the ashram, having heard of the greatness of His father. She sat before Sri Gurudev and asked, "Where can I find such a teacher?" After several minutes, the woman left, no wiser. The living Sage would never say that he was what she sought. If she was earnest, she would have seen. How different this is from the massive publicity and ambition one witnesses today!

A total novice and at the beginning, I would twice or thrice daily attend the Sage. (It was not a public ashram. One had to seek permission first.) He never lectured, but as Socrates, waited to be asked questions then responded. If no questions, then He simply sat in silence, and this in itself was powerful. If one were open, the energy transmission was sweet and overwhelming. One night, I sat alone with the Teacher, and no questions arose. Finally, I said, "I don't have any questions. Is it all right if I just stay and look into your eyes?" Modestly, He replied, "Yes."

Another time, I wanted urgently to see Him but He was not available. I waited impatiently in the Talk Room then fell to the floor in another epileptic seizure as I had experienced several times since a small child — as had my father before me. At that very moment, He appeared and, though He had never before touched me, laid his hand upon my head, firmly holding it there for some time. Soon all was calm. And that was the last grand mal seizure I ever had. (When I returned to the States two years later, Raja suggested I return to the same doctor who had before given me the EEG brain test which clearly showed the epilepsy. I did return to the same doctor who took another EEG, and comparing the two tests, was at a loss to explain. My brain was completely normal!)

Later Sri Gurudev explained that a Guru will not show his powers unless it is necessary for a disciple's spiritual advancement. My condition would have proven a handicap to experiencing the higher levels.

On one occasion, I was becoming frustrated attending the twice daily devotional ritual where His father's ashes were interred. My frustration was, "Why should I bow to ashes when a living Guru is here?" One night, I slipped away during the ritual and entered from the back of the house to where I knew my Teacher would be quietly sitting in his chair in the Talk Room. I silently entered the room and saw an amazing sight! As Sri Gurudev was meditating, bathed in a bright white light, His form grew larger than life, filling the entire room, then shrank to an extremely small size as He dissolved totally into the Light. Trembling, my eyes full of tears, for the first time, I prostrated on the floor before the Guru. After this, I would go every night to prostrate while others were attending the nightly ritual bowing before the ashes. Little by little, other Westerners would do the same. At a later date, after reading the *Bhagavad Gita*, I read a description of Krishna revealing his true Self to Arjuna, his disciple, and it was described exactly as I had witnessed that evening.

Krishna with Arjuna

Twice a day, Sri Gurudev would walk to the river and bathe. One afternoon, I was walking by the river and happened to see Him standing in the river, bathing. Unnoticed by Him, two white doves flew in continuous circles directly above His head. It was an amazing sight! Then to see Him walking back from the river, sprinkling water from his jug as the sages of old might have done, including the eighth-century Kerala sage, Sri Shankara, who had lived and taught less than an hour from this very village! All is timeless in this sacred place.

Once during a special ritual for His father and Guru, I lost consciousness and fell to the ground. Others approached to try and rouse me. Sri Gurudev appeared and said to them, "No, don't touch her. Don't wake her." After a few moments, I came to, having experienced a special vision showing that true sages would always be there from one to another, as long as sincere seekers exist.

This began the week when I was unable to eat anything. I was not ill, only full of Light from the atmosphere. I disappeared upstairs to a secluded room where I had received permission to meditate. This time, I had the deepest conviction that I had achieved my reason to live and that the quest of many lives had been fulfilled. So, I sat cross-legged on the floor in deep meditation in order to leave the body once and for all. In Samadhi (transcendental state), I felt the kundalini rising upward as a serpent from the base of the spine. I somehow knew that when it reached and exited the top of my head, all would be over. At this moment, the door behind me opened and I felt the Guru's presence. I knew I should stand but could not move. He quickly crossed the room and for the second time, put his hand upon my head and with great force pushed me down, preventing the kundalini from exiting my head. I prostrated full bodied and touched His Feet. For some reason, I did not prostrate as a woman with bended knees as usual, but as a man, fully stretched upon the ground. The Sage gently told me, "This is not our way." Then He bade me to go downstairs. Soon he came and instructed his wife to feed me. I was seated in the dining room where I always ate directly across from my Teacher when Sri Gurudev's wife brought a green banana leaf then served rice and yogurt as my Guru stood nearby and gestured for me to eat. It was extremely difficult after the week of fasting, but I slowly ate what was before me. And I never attempted to leave the body again.

At another time, I was awakened at night with the distinct feeling that Sri Gurudev was in peril of some kind. I hurriedly walked to His home. He came out and said all was well. I told him I felt His life was being threatened. He understood my psychic tendencies yet never encouraged them. In the same way, when I tried to ask him about past lives as I knew I had known Him before, He would evade. I persisted and He finally said, "It's difficult enough to transcend one life. Why bring in all the others?"

This same week I went to bathe in the holy river as usual about 6 A.M. It was the beginning of the monsoon and the waters were a bit turbulent due to the heavy rains. I was bathing near the tall river weeds that grew up from the river bed and felt something move at my feet. Thinking it was just some river debris, I shook my foot then felt something slither up inside my clothes to my chin as a small black snake jumped straight up to the sky and into the river. Though not large, it was a very poisonous snake. Later I asked Him, "Why was I not bitten?" And He replied, "Because you were holding on to Me and protected." Three days later, in late morning as I walked to His house, I spied a five-foot cobra slowly turning a corner, heading toward the front porch. Serpents are very sensitive to psychic atmospheres and, at this time, the atmosphere was extremely strong as good triumphed over evil.

There is a certain ruthlessness about Advaita Vedanta, a lack of humanity, or so I have sometimes felt. Indians walking by dying people on the road with the thought, "That is their karma. Nothing to do with me." Some years later, there was an American couple with a small boy of about five who came to live in the ashram. As a mother, I felt concerned as the couple tended to neglect their child. I had hired an ayah to care for Christopher when I was attending the Talks. Tropical India was an ongoing challenge for all of us to stay well. For instance, one must never go barefoot due to hook worms which enter through the feet. So, I made sure that my son always wore his buckled plastic sandals.

One day, returning from Sri Gurudev's home, I spotted the young American boy sitting alone as usual, but noticed he seemed too still, blankly staring into space. As I came closer, I saw a multitude of small live white hook worms crawling from his mouth. Upset, I hurried to the main house and finding the parents, urged them to take their son to the Clinic twenty minutes away. Their casual reply was, "Oh, he'll be all right. Gurudev is looking out for him." My response to this 'magical thinking' was anger. I turned and though it was not my business, obtained an auto-rikshaw and took the boy at once to the clinic. The Christian doctor who had saved my life treated him and later told me that had I waited another day the boy would have surely died.

Of course, perhaps it is not the Vedanta philosophy to blame but rather how some — both Indians and Westerners — sometimes interpret the teaching. Sri Gurudev was a caring father to His children and once told me that it was good that I looked after my own son so well. In any case, I vowed then and there that I would never sacrifice my humanity or concern for others for my spiritual life.

I continued to write in my journals only if and when the writing came of itself.

> Try and be a sheet of paper with nothing on it.
> Be a spot of ground where nothing is growing,
> Where something might be planted,
> A seed, possibly from the Absolute.
> Stop the words now.
> Open the window in the center of your chest,

And let the spirits fly in and out.

Sri Nisargadatta Maharaj

Slowly more and more seekers appeared from the West. This period was an intense time and there were many inexplicable incidents. And also, later on, through those who had met Him, some extraordinary individuals came to the Sage. I was always thankful that unlike many groups surrounding spiritual teachers who seemed like cookie cutter imitations of their teacher, it was the opposite here. Each remained entirely individual and the goal was to go authentically to the end of yourself. This being said, there remained great diversity.

One amazing American was Jory. She had lived for years in India, mostly New Delhi, as her husband was head of Coca Cola for all of South Asia. Her husband did not share his wife's fascination with the spiritual which led eventually to their divorce. Jory came with her two young children, Zora and Tom, and stayed in the ashram for some months. She was intense and manic-depressive; today she would be called bipolar. The Sage asked me to look after Jory as she was mentally unstable at this time.

A gifted poet, she was sometimes mad, always generous, and had a great sense of humor. Once I spied Jory sitting in a chair under the mango tree near the Sage's home as two tall Indian servants/disciples, Prem and Arjun stood on either side of her. They knew not a word of English and there Jory sat reading aloud to them in her strong dramatic voice, Shakespeare's *Julius Cesar*.

Jory purchased the first telephone in the village as a gift for our Teacher. He did not want it in the house so it was installed in a small two-room house next to the big house. The moment came when it rang. Our Teacher stood just outside his room and told Adeep, a faithful servant and disciple of His father, to answer the phone when it rang. Hesitantly, Adeep picked up the receiver and holding it some six inches in front of his face, said, "Hello? Hello?" then turned to the Sage and said "Not working." We all gestured to him to hold the phone to his ear which eventually he did. All laughed and laughed.

Adeep, a retired water engineer, was a disciple of Sri Gurudev's father. After he retired, he came to serve the son of his Guru, and one of his duties was to light the camphor and incense each evening. Though a modest and simple man, he possessed a hidden depth. He helped me in many ways as well, teaching me Malayalam, the local language, which is seventy-five percent Sanskrit. There were at that time no text books in English so we used first grade textbooks — all written entirely in Malayalam. I should add that at this time, the language was written without separating the words which made it a greater challenge to learn! Malayalam is one of twenty-two official languages in India and has almost twice the number of letters as does the English alphabet. I struggled to learn to read, write, and speak the language of my Teacher. The Sage's wife would tease me, "Malayalam is not so difficult. Look how well your son speaks it and he is only three years old!"

Jory continued to be a problem. Some days she could be lucid yet another day, she might be mad again.

One day Jory was in a very bad way so I followed her to the river. Jory marched with purpose into the river and entered the middle where the current is strongest. Then she abruptly fell face down into the river. There was no doubt as to her intention. I dived in and swam to her. Luckily, as I had learned in Life Saving class years before, I attempted to hold her from behind. Jory shouted, "You must leave. Go. Go." Ignoring her, I carried her in with much difficulty, wrenching my back in the process. Now Jory was six-foot-tall and very strong — more so when she was in her manic state. Later she was furious with me for interfering. Sri Gurudev saw that her heart was pure so there was never a thought to send her away. Thankfully, she did not try this again, and gradually her sanity returned.

Twenty-four years later when I moved from New York to Los Angeles then to Ojai, I got in touch with Jory who was totally well by then and living in Santa Barbara. We renewed our friendship as though no time had passed. I never mentioned the near drowning incident in India years before as I assumed that she did not remember, not being in her right mind then. However, early one evening in my back garden in Ojai, we were watching the sunset — the 'famous' Ojai pink moment that often appears once the sun has gone to rest. The silence was full as we were both thinking of the Sage. Suddenly, out of the silence and without looking at me, Jory said, "I've been meaning to thank you, Catherine, for saving my life in India so many years ago. It turned out to be a good one after all."

"I wasn't sure you remembered that day."

"Yes, I do."

Surprised and moved, I said nothing. What was there to say? We sat silently for some time watching the pink sky, and it was never mentioned again.

Jory became a firm friend of many years, and continued to write splendid poetry. Our last meeting occurred in a swank nursing home in Santa Barbara. A photograph of our Teacher was placed near her bed. Knowing how she loved good chocolate, I had brought some fine dark chocolate and asked, "Should I put it in your drawer?" Jory quickly responded, "Do I have to wait?" I laughed and said, "No, of course not." Then we shared some of the chocolate. Jory ate it slowly, closing her eyes in utter enjoyment. Three days later, she was gone.

And then there was the incredible Irina. I had first met

Irina in Paris on my wedding trip with Raja. Irina was my age then, twenty, and told me, "I wish I could be marrying an Indian!" In Paris, she had been an actress with the Living Theatre group, co-founded by Judith Malina and Julian Beck. The Living Theatre was a radical political theatre troupe that rose to prominence in New York City and Paris during the 1950s and 60s. Her mother, Nadia, was a follower of Gurdieff, the Russian mystic, so Irina was unconventionally raised among the Gurdieff group. A few years later, she was also living in the ashram and we became friends.

The first year Irina came to the ashram was during Jory's mad time, and I was concerned for Jory's young children. It was Christmas week and my mother had sent several gifts for my son. I told her that we should have a Christmas Party for the children. Our music teacher, Bhavani, offered her own home for the occasion. We decorated the house with Christmas cards, wrapped gifts, and bought sweets in a nearby town. I also invited my Teacher's children who were then in their early teens. The party was a great success and I was delighted to see Jory's children not only smile but laugh as they opened their gifts and ate the sweets. Adeep surprised us all by singing the song, *Jingle Bells* — in English. Then Irina lit sparklers and did a modern twirling dance outside with them. Martha Graham would have been impressed! We all returned to our beds, tired yet happy.

The next morning, I was sent for by Sri Gurudev. He asked me about the Christmas Party. I smiled and said, "It was just a party for the children. No religion or anything." He said his daughter told him there was a picture of Mother Virgin. I laughed and said, "You mean the Virgin Mary? No. Oh, maybe on one of the Christmas cards we decorated the room with." Well, I never lived that one down. Years later, Sri Gurudev in front of the many disciples that would later come, would turn to me and exclaim, "She had a Christmas Party for my children and Mother Virgin was there!"

Encouraged by our Teacher, we began singing lessons with Bhavani, a disciple of His Father as well as a professional Carnatic singer. (Carnatic is the classical music of south India.) Impatient to learn kirtanams (devotional songs) as sung daily after sunset, we had to struggle through the Carnatic scales for what seemed like forever. Finally, we learned Sanskrit slokas (verses) and devotional songs written by Sri Shankara, and others.

Years later, in the mid-1980s, I had arranged for a Vedic architect and builder to build a house near the ashram, in the same traditional Kerala style as our Teacher's home though much smaller — a two-storied stone house with a red tile sloping roof and two separate bedrooms and baths downstairs and upstairs with a large terrace which served as a family living room. Christopher especially loved the teak swing based on models from ancient times in Kerala usually seen in palaces of the kings of long ago. In addition, we purchased two Kerala-styled wooden leisure chairs with canvas seats where we could lie back as in a lawn chair and read or talk, and a large round green marble table and plastic chairs where we had our meals on the upstairs terrace.

For some years, having outgrown the small Talk Room at the front of His home, we had the Talks on the front porch. Behind His chair was an exquisitely carved wooden screen to keep out drafts. There was one male peacock who would daily fly and land on top of the wooden screen, perched just over the Sage's head, and sit there silently during the talks. I was convinced that this was an old soul reincarnated. At a much later date, on the day Sri Gurudev passed away, they found the peacock dead, on the floor directly in front of His chair.

Once while standing alone with the Sage, I was outspoken, even disrespectful when speaking to Him. He said firmly, "You must leave this place. Go back to America."

Shocked, I turned and left. It was late at night and very dark. Where could I go? In the darkness, I walked to the river with a clear intent to end my life. If denied my Teacher's presence, there is no meaning in living. I walked down the steep steps to the dark waters below. Pausing only a brief moment, I jumped in letting the current pull me to oblivion. Then I heard Bill, a disciple from Texas, call out. "Come. You must come. He is asking for you."

I swam back to the steps, got out, dripping, and walked towards the ashram.

Suddenly, aware of my state, I thought, "I can't go before the Guru in these wet clothes." So, I walked to my room, quickly put on a dry sari and then walked to Sri Gurudev's home. Before Him, I prostrated then stood quietly, at Home again. He had brought me Home. Then gently, calmly, He related a story from the Upanishads which I did not know. A disciple had been disrespectful to his Guru and the Guru ordered him to leave. The disciple went at once to the nearby river and proceeded to drown himself. The teacher came after him, and held him down, saying, "This is how you must desire the Truth, as a drowning man gasping for breath." There was never any mention of this again. Lesson learned.

During those first two years living in the ashram, Sri Gurudev was invited to Cairo as there were disciples there. I decided to stay for the two weeks He was away. Though challenging, I was unprepared for what occurred. Prem, the tall servant whom Jory had read Shakespeare's *Julius Cesar* to, was tragically bitten by a large cobra.

They carried his six-foot tall body to the cement stage

next to the Family's Home. I was the only Westerner there and with my elementary Malayalam urged them to get a taxi and take him to the kind Christian doctor in the nearest town, some twenty minutes away. Instead, they sent for a Brahmin priest who mumbled some Sanskrit slokas over his body. After a few minutes as the poor lad writhed in pain, he raised up his head and swooned in a circular movement resembling a serpent, then laid back down and lost consciousness. Assuming he was dead, I returned to my cottage, learning only much later that he was taken to the clinic and died there a few days later. Some days passed before I was told that he was attacked by the cobra because he violated the snake shrine. Before Sri Gurudev's father and Guru had purchased the land, it was a jungle and at the time, a home to many poisonous serpents. After the site was cleared and the house built, they created an enclosed area and a serpent shrine. No one was allowed to enter the shrine as it was for the serpents only. The night before his death, Prem had gone there and lain with Prisha, a house servant — thus polluting the shrine. For this, the cobra killed him. This, too, is India.

I was relieved when Sri Gurudev returned from Egypt, and all was as before. The hours daily spent sitting before the Sage with questions or simply the darshan of utter shining silence filling my heart was all I could desire.

I had thought then to remain forever in India. Yet after

two momentous years, my Teacher gently nudged me out of the spiritual nest, instructing me that I must follow my dharma (the inner law of one's existence). He said I was to return to the work I had begun before (the theatre) and also return to my marriage. He cited a saying that even after enlightenment, *the prarabdha karmas* must continue rather like the cock (rooster) after his head is cut off, he goes on dancing. (Prarabdha Karmas are the results of past actions from a previous life affecting the current one and drives what we do or think).

I told Him that I would die if I had to leave! Then I sat under the mango tree and wept and wept. Amma, the wife of Sri Gurudev, came and sat next to me.

"Why are you crying?"

"I want to be a sannyasini." (One who renounces the world, a female nun.)

Amma laughed and said, "But you have husband and child. How can you be a sannyasini!"

Of course, the Sage knew me better than I knew myself and He knew what lay ahead as well. The years lived there by the sacred river were indeed a blessing of the gods. I see now that this time away from life as usual became a foundation of all that was to follow. Stripped of all that was familiar, it enabled me to sink deeper into myself. India is a mirror which intensifies whatever is reflected within. This wonder that is India shall ever remain deep in the inner geography of my heart. Sri Gurudev's parting words to me were:

The realization of the Truth is in the living of it.

The way back to Self is not an easy journey but the only one worth making. To view one's life symbolically and not literally is to discover meaning at each step. It is a never-ending story. Though individual in detail, the archetypal patterns are universal, ever changing, and unlike dogma or religion, its forms are as varied and as changeless as the sea. The journey that began at age four seeing the Kamakura Buddha in Japan — my first glimpse of God — carried me to south India, and through the grace of the Guru, the awakening of the Self that is One with Truth.

C. G. Jung left Sigmund Freud and a promising career as his heir apparent, and began a four-year retreat. He lived in solitude, drew and painted (*The Red Book*), later remarking that these years were the most important of his life, and that from them came the foundation of all that came later. Looking back, I see this first trip to India as a similar period for me. These intense two years remain the most important of my life, providing the strength that would accompany me for the rest of my days.

It was 1970 and the world 'it was a changing' as Bob

Dylan sang. After wearing a sari for two years in south India, I experienced reverse culture shock seeing women's dress lines high above the knees! It was, as well, an exciting time. Students were thirsty for Truth and over three hundred of them would attend Raja's classes in Austin — an example of what was happening in America. Many of them were truly seekers at heart. I remember one particular class in Austin. I stood at the back in a large hall where enthralled students filled the aisles, standing on the side or in the back when there were no more seats to be had. The Civil Rights movement was in full sway as were the anti-Viet Nam War protests. Disenchantment with the government was rampant. At one point in Raja's class in Austin at the University of Texas, an intense young man cried out, "Why shouldn't I kill myself?" A hush filled the hall as Raja Rao answered, "Yes, that is exactly what I want you to do. Only the real suicide: the death of the ego." The silence in the hall was deafening as they understood that it is the ego — not the body — that must die. And the young man so desperate a moment ago, smiled as light shone on his face. Some of these students found their way through Raja to the small village in Kerala where I had spent the last two years, becoming disciples of the Householder Sage, Sri Gurudev — including two of my former professors. Though my husband never openly spoke or encouraged the students during class, several would show up at his office door, wanting more, and with persistence would find their way to India and the Feet of the Sage.

Out of respect to the Sage and His Family, I do not reveal His real name or place. Though Sri Gurudev did not give public talks or publicly open the ashram, many came via other disciples. For the next four decades, I returned each year with Christopher and sometimes with Raja to Kerala, to what would remain our spiritual home.

My son, Christopher, and I in our India home

On our annual visit to India when Christopher was five, he asked if he could see Sri Gurudev alone to ask a question. It was granted and I was told to stand near the door. Then my son walked closer to the Sage, and stood there, unable to speak. The

Sage said, "You have something to ask me?" Then, summoning courage, Christopher spoke:

"Is there anything beyond time?

"Any true experience is always beyond time."

"What is time?"

"Time is only a thought."

Satisfied, Christopher, with folded hands, bowed to his Guru and quietly left the room. I was touched that the Sage responded to this five-year-old in the same manner as to any adult disciple.

On my way back one year to New York from Kerala, I stopped overnight in Bombay (now Mumbai). I was walking near the Taj Hotel passing a church close to the Gate of India. I looked inside the courtyard and saw an elderly holy man sitting on the front steps of the church. He abruptly stood up as if he knew me and greeted me with a namaste. Though it was evening and quite dark, I felt safe so I walked towards the older Indian. He surprised me by saying, "You have come from Malabar." Malabar is the ancient name for Kerala. Then he astounded me by saying the name of my Teacher's father and guru! Putting my palms together, I said to him, "I have just come from His Son." Somehow, he had felt the energy of my Teacher and his own Guru, and we experienced a lovely, long, and deep moment. Though we never met again, I would forever remember the power of the Guru's Presence.

Sri Gurudev was invited privately to travel to the west once a year rotating with Paris, France one year and the United States the alternate year, initially to Maryland near Washington DC, and later to Austin, Texas as there were so many of us there. I attended three of the Paris Talks and all of the many American Talks over the next three decades.

When in the West, He would always wear western clothes so as not to stand out. Once during one of the Talks in France, held in Senlis just outside of Paris, I sat on the floor along with some two hundred or more disciples. I rarely asked questions now but simply opened my heart to receive. At one moment, I saw a bright shining white light glow from the chest of the Guru and then rays reaching out to many of us in the gathering. One ray penetrated my heart, taking my breath away.

Many years later, after His Passing in 2001, I was in Kerala and visited the Large Talk Room that had been built as the number of followers grew. On the platform next to where the Sage would sit in a large chair, stood a portrait of Him that one of the French disciples had painted. I began to meditate on the painting as it was a realistic likeness of our Teacher. The room was dark with no lights on and no light coming through the windows. Suddenly I saw a bright circular light manifest in the middle of His chest exactly as I had also seen in Paris. I had a camera with me and took a photograph to be sure I was seeing correctly. Later back in the States, I had it developed and it showed a close up of the painting with the bright, circular white light in the middle of His chest which was not in the original painting! Surrounding the Sage, these are not unusual occurrences, as sometimes they would occur daily. Still, these manifestations remain a blessing — especially after the Sage left the body.

Years before, Sri Gurudev told me something that I did not comprehend at the time. In a private talk, I had asked Him, "What happens after the Guru leaves the body? What happens to the relationship?"

"The Guru-disciple relationship will become even stronger."

Apart from attending the Talks in the west, I would for the next forty-one years travel back each year to Kerala, to the Sage. My life became a pendulum swinging between acting and writing in New York and Hollywood then withdrawing to the ashram in Kerala. *Buddha and the Dancing Girl* continued to be the archetypal motif for my life for many years, alternating between spiritual practice and creative expression.

Sri Gurudev knew me well and nudging me out of the spiritual nest was the right choice — though it would take a long while to fully accept that this was so. If not in India, I knew I had no choice but to follow my creative passion and return to the theatre. The dance of karma would continue, and in my case, this meant returning to New York.

> We never stay the same person.
> We change as we grow old.
> The things that happen to us
> make us different people.
> It's part of the story of our life.
>
> William Boyd, *Any Human Heart*

Part IV Lure of the Greasepaint
New York, 1970-1989

I've got something in me,

I don't know what,

That wants to soar.

Rimbaud

Catherine, 26

During the early years of our marriage, I was content to set aside

my aspirations in order to be wife and mother to this amazing man I had wed. This was no sacrifice as the marriage was bliss at this stage. I felt no separation from my husband, as I had for the first time experienced a total surrender to my feminine self. Then pulled to India by a longing for the spiritual, I had lived for two years away from Raja — except for one visit when he came to India after a year to see if I was ready to return. I stayed on in the ashram another year and would have remained longer had my Teacher not nudged me out of the nest.

Now, after a sojourn in Austin, my husband and I continued a commuting marriage — commuting between Austin, New York, Paris, and India. Separation was not easy as love was there, but I knew myself well enough to know that if I did not pursue what was so strongly in me, the theatre, I would not be a very good wife or mother. Luckily, my husband agreed. Although he did not offer financial support, he said I should try and live my dream, or otherwise I might always regret it. I had already agreed that Raja should teach only one semester instead of two in order to have more time to write his novels. So, since this meant only half his original salary, money was scarce. And I had already exhausted my small inheritance from my father on the two years in India. Much later, I realized that Raja had hoped I would try and fail then return full time to the marriage. However, this was not to be the case.

My agent, Barna Ostertag, was an old friend and

colleague of B. Iden Payne, mentor from my college days. She told me that in all the decades of their friendship, Payne had only referred one other actor to her, Barbara Barrie. Barrie was awarded Best Actress at the Cannes Film Festival in 1964 and later known for her portrayal of the wife to television series detective *Barney Miller*. Thereupon, Barna signed me on the spot and began to arrange auditions for me. During the run of *The Happy Haven*, Barna had set up an audition for an upcoming Broadway show that had been a recent hit on the West End in London, *Rosencrantz and Guildenstern*. And when I told her I would instead be going to India with my husband and son, she simply said, "Call me when you return." Two years later I made that call and began my acting career in earnest.

Most of my first acting jobs were playing leading roles in regional theatres so I would be for two months in Cincinnati or Florida or wherever. Between acting jobs, I would substitute teach in various schools. I have always found that when there is a clear calling, regardless of the risks, somehow things work out.

A friend of Raja's and mine, Violette Verdy, had found a studio apartment for me, just around the corner from her own flat where she and her mother, Jeanne, lived. Our apartments were near Lincoln Center where Violette performed as prima ballerina in the New York City Ballet.

Violette Verdy (1933-2016)

Violette invited me to see *Jewels*, a ballet created for her and two other great ballerinas. *Emeralds* was the one Balanchine had created for her. It was superb. As I watched the ballet that evening at Lincoln Center, I saw white subtle spirits floating above the dancers, and thought surely only a genius could create such a work to manifest ethereal spirits. Backstage, I told Violette what I saw, and, with her adorable French accent, she immediately said, "Oh, *Cat-treen*, you must tell him. You must tell him now!" She then introduced me to George Balanchine and I told him what I had witnessed. He nodded, not surprised, and simply said, "It is natural." Then he graciously invited me to attend rehearsals whenever I liked. The following week, I did so. It was an extraordinary experience to silently watch this master creating a new ballet. The dancers were as moist clay in his hand. He would become very still, stare blankly, suddenly take an arm or a torso then twirl or shape it. Observing the sculptor Rodin at work would probably have been a similar experience.

George Balanchine

Later Balanchine invited a few of us for supper at his apartment on the Upper West Side near Lincoln Center. There I watched the maestro cook in the same fashion in which he had choreographed. No cookbooks were needed. His concentration and delight were the same. Here was a creative life. Later after a sumptuous gourmet dinner, his cat performed for us. Yes, Balanchine had taught the cat to dance!

What struck me was that in Balanchine's mind, all of life was a creative experience. There was no separation between life and art.

The gift of Art rests in the artist's perspective.

Journal 1970

One time when Violette had just returned from a NY City Ballet Tour of Russia, Poland, and Paris, she invited me to have dinner. At the Opera de 'Paris, Violette had just performed *Giselle* to raves! I mentioned seeing our mutual friend and superb concert pianist, Madeline Malraux, widow of Andre Malraux, a close friend of Raja's, who played Stravinsky's *Circus Polka* at a well-received Paris concert recently. Over dinner, Violette asked me, "Do you know the story? Sometime ago when Balanchine did not yet have his own company, he had to make a living. Barnum & Bailey asked him if he would choreograph a dance for their elephants. Balanchine telephoned his friend, Igor Stravinsky, and asked him if he would write something for a dance for elephants. Without the slightest hesitation, Stravinsky replied, "How old are the elephants?" Balanchine replied, "Very young ones. "Hence the "Circus

Polka" was born!

Every artist must spend some years in New York City, if for no other reason, than the amazing, creative people one meets. Though India is my spiritual home, New York formed me creatively.

It was not a smooth transition to leave a protective, spiritual enclave for a sometimes-ruthless metropolis like Manhattan. Once acting in an off-Broadway show, I was returning late from rehearsal, and felt very homesick for my Teacher and His family. Riding in an empty subway car, I began to cry and inwardly reached out for Sri Gurudev. The subway doors opened and a middle-aged south Indian couple entered the train. Though the car was empty, they came near, and the husband sat on one side of me and the wife on the other. I continued to weep out loud, even sob. The couple never said a word yet somehow their proximity consoled me. After several minutes, the car stopped and they left as silently as they had come. Through them, I felt the distinct presence of my Teacher.

> Persistent striving is necessary,
> but once one is There,
> there is no other place to go.
>
> Sri Gurudev

I auditioned and was cast as understudy for the role of

Anna Karenina plus all the lesser women's parts in *Anna K*, a New York production and a fine adaptation of Tolstoy's novel by Eugenie Leontovich, actress and director. Leontovich had starred in *Anastasia* on Broadway years before. Now an Equity Union actor, I first began to learn the lesser parts and later planned to learn the leading role. Fate intervened and the leading lady fell ill before I had learned her part! This allowed only twenty-four hours to learn all her lines and staging. I called on friends to come over and hold book and cue me. Each friend would stay one or two hours. The next night when I was due to go on, I went early to the theatre to learn the blocking. Before curtain that night, I did a meditation, asking for my Teacher's support. The show went very well or so I was told later. Actually, I remember only the opening line I spoke then nothing at all, until the curtain call at the end of the play where I received a standing ovation. It was as if I was carried through the entire performance in a magical, dreamlike experience, myself disappearing and the character taking over totally. It could not have gone better. Later a producer approached, introduced himself then asked how I got my eyes to shine so brightly. (No doubt I had help from India!) The leading lady recovered, was released, and I was asked to take over the lead. Funny thing, I continued to play Anna for the run of the show, eight performances a week, and though it went well, I don't think I ever rose to that opening night performance again.

This happened to me a second time when I was later cast as understudy for Juliet in Shakespeare's *Romeo and Juliet,* another NY production. The actress dropped out before I had time to learn the lines. Again, I called upon my friends to take shifts holding script so I could learn more quickly. I was fortunate in that I learned lines quickly though as soon as a show ended, the memory of those lines was totally wiped. All was well and I was asked to continue the run of the show as Juliet. Needless to say, my earlier training with Shakespearean director, B. Iden Payne, helped enormously! Also, at thirty-four, I figured it was my last chance to play a fourteen-year-old! Jeanne Campbell, Lord Beaverbrook's granddaughter and former wife of novelist Norman Mailer, played the Nurse, and was wonderful. Jeanne was — even off-stage — an Elizabethan character, and we later became good friends.

Even though I had been frightened while studying acting with Lee Strasberg during my earlier stay in NY, I auditioned for Uta Hagen's class and began studying with her at her husband's H.B. Studio in Greenwich Village. From my exper-ience, she was the finest teacher in NY at that time. A brilliant actress herself, she was known for her Desdemona on Broadway opposite Paul Robeson's Othello. She had also originated the role of Martha in Edward Albee's *Who's Afraid of Virginia*

Woolf? which I had seen when I was seventeen. The wonderful thing about Uta Hagen was she never played the 'star'. It was an acting lab and our total focus was on 'the work'. When I auditioned with Ophelia from *Hamlet,* she told me, "I want you to play an Ophelia who goes to the bathroom!" At first, I was shocked as I had pride in my Shakespearean training thanks to B. Iden Payne, former director of Stratford-on-Avon. Later, I realized that her technique grounded me, making my characters more real. Later on, I was asked to teach Voice and Diction at her studio so joined the faculty. I heard it once said that the best acting lies in the middle of the ocean between NY and London. In other words, both outer and inner technique are necessary.

I felt at home playing the Greek classics as I did Shakespeare or Tolstoy. I did have one problem though. After performances playing the classical roles, it would take me longer to come back to earth in order to sleep. It was, as if in order to play such roles, you had to become bigger than you were. To research Cassandra, the priestess in *The Trojan Woman*, I went to the Metropolitan Art Museum to study the figures painted on the Greek vases. This suggested the movements of the ancient Greeks. At the times when Cassandra foretold what would happen during the Trojan War, I played her as a psychic. I would first become completely still, silent, then, facing full front toward the audience, actually see a vision of the future, and only then commence the monologue, describing the tragedy soon to unfold. An actor must draw on all she has, and psychic since childhood, it felt right to play her in that fashion. Also, I could more easily relate and become her.

Cassandra in *The Trojan Women*, NY, 1970-71

At a friend's suggestion, I visited Ethel Myers, a known psychic, then in her late sixties, who lived on the upper West side not far from my place. She looked like an ordinary grandmother and said many things to me about the future — most of them long forgotten until years later after I had moved to California, I found the audio tape. Myers foresaw that I would stop acting and have even more success writing. She also predicted that I would later work in Hollywood. Interesting that she saw all this decades before any thought arose of going to Hollywood! She revealed one more insight that I found quite interesting. She said that in playing so many diverse roles as an actor, I would not have to return to live those lives. I cannot swear that this is so, but on some level, it made perfect sense to me, as my approach to creating the parts was to become and live them fully, so that afterwards, I was freed in some way. For instance, both Juliet and Anna Karenina had killed themselves, so it was comforting to know," been there, done that'.

In *La Fiesta*, I played Lilian Roth's granddaughter. I do not recall the characters name and the play was not memorable except for playing with the former singer and Hollywood star, Miss Roth. She is remembered for starring in *Animal Crackers* with the Marx Brothers as well as for her bestselling auto-biography, *I'll Cry Tomorrow* about Lilian's battle with alcholism.. Her book became a Hollywood blockbuster film with the same title, and Susan Hayward was nominated for an Oscar for portraying Lilian. Lilian, very conscious of having been a star, caried both a certain dignity as well as a revealing sense of her past struggles.

La Fiesta with Lilian Roth, NY

I was cast in Edward Albee's play, *A Delicate Balance,* with rehearsals to start at the Cincinatti Playhouse in six weeks. The role of Julia was a good one and I was delighted. Also as it was time for my annual pilgrimage to India, this meant work would be waiting for me when I returned.

One day, Violette called me, forlorn, to say she had broken her foot. In tears, she added, "I cannot dance for six weeks!" Imagine her surprise when I responded, "That's great." Shocked, she said, "What! *Cat-treen*, why is that great?" 'Because I am leaving for India next week and you can come with me!" Violette had expressed for a long time her desire to meet my Teacher. Well, she did come, limping but enthusiastic. And it was a wonderful trip for her. At my suggestion, she chose to undergo the ancient Auryvedic treatment which meant that her cast was broken and she endured daily wet mud and herb wraps followed by Auyvedic massage. Auyveda, an ancient system of medicine, originated in Kerala. The result? She was walking normally in two weeks! Soon after, she would don her practice leotards and dance. We invited Sri Gurudev and His family to watch one day, as they had never seen Classical Ballet. When Violette jumped high into the air then fell to the cement floor in a perfect split, Gurudev's wife, exclaimed, "Oh, she will break!"

It was mid-winter. I travelled from tropical India to a wintry, snowy Cincinatti, complete with jetlag. Having purchased at the airport bookstore, *A Hundred Years of Solitude*

Julia in *A Delicate Balance*

by Gabriel Garcia Marquez, I could not for the life of me stop reading it. The result was I dragged through the early rehearsals due to jetlag and was the last to learn my lines. The director, Hal Scott, began to have doubts about having cast me in NYC several weeks before. Fortunately, I quickly finished the great novel, overcame the jetlag, line perfect, and the play was a great success. It was a wonderful company, too, with Carolyn Coates and James Noble (*Benson,* the television series,1979-1985), and Jill Andre (*The Trip Back Home* on Broadway with John Cullum). I played Julia, their daughter and niece, returning home after my fourth marriage had failed, having a nervous breakdown, then trying to shoot my parents. Good stuff, what!

Julia in final scene in *A Delicate Balance*

Cincinatti Playhouse received their best notices ever and I was offered a role in their next production, *Long Day's Journey into Night* by Eugene O'Neill. As it was a small part, I declined — also because it was just too cold in Ohio!

Every actor knows that no matter the success, a show's run eventually ends and there is *the in-between* to deal with — being a freelance for hire. Between acting gigs, I would substitute teach as I had my high school teaching certificate from The University of Texas. I would also work for Louis Harris, the market research agency. This job was rather interesting as it varied each day. I would go personally to whomever was targeted to answer a questionnaire administered by workers such as myself. It paid well and when I got an acting job, I could quit and return later, if needed. I interviewed CEOs to mob guys working in the meat market.

One day, Suzanne, an actress friend of mine from Texas now living in NYC, suggested I wait tables in a fancy restaurant where she worked on the east side. I told her I had never done that before, but she waived my reservations aside, informing her boss that I was experienced. It was lunchtime at the Kitty Hawk Restaurant on Madison Avenue, and the clientele were mostly business men. My first challenge was serving the cocktails. I had never had alcohol so knew nothing of cocktails. I had a tray of six drinks and had to interrupt the customers saying, "Hmm, who ordered the red drink?" As if this wasn't bad enough, when I brought the lunch, one man had ordered the large butterfly shrimp. When I bent over, the fried shrimp slid off the plate straight into the 3-piece suited businessman's lap! His face was so funny that I unfortunately burst out laughing! That's when I got fired.

Next, I opted for secretarial temp work. I was sent to a Chemical Research company and asked to type pages and pages of chemical names and numbered formulas which were Greek to me. I kept leaving for the restroom as it became so tedious, I thought I would scream. By the end of the day, it was noticed that I had inadvertently skipped one line so that all the following pages and pages of formulas that I had typed did not tally. That's when I got fired.

The very next day I had an audition for a Broadway revival of Arthur Miller's *Death of a Salesman* with actor George C. Scott directing. I told myself that I had better get this job as I couldn't do much of anything else.

An artist is someone who can't do anything else.

Jasper Johns

As Hollywood star, Teresa Wright, was already cast to play the wife of Willy Loman, I auditioned for a supporting role appearing in only two scenes. Surprised, I read for George C.

Scott (*Patton*) himself. The very next day, Barna Ostertag — still my agent — called to say I got the part! We would rehearse in NYC then first open in Philadelphia at the Walnut Theatre — where Sarah Bernhardt and Eleonora Duse had played — before bringing *Salesman* to Broadway. After two weeks of intense rehearsals in a studio in the middle of the Broadway district, we packed and headed for Philadelphia. We soon learned why comic actor W. C. Fields put on his tombstone, "This beats playing Philadelphia!" For starters, in the seventies, it was difficult to find a good restaurant open late at night, after doing a show. Actors, as a rule, eat light before curtain, and afterwards, are ravenous.

One Monday night when we had time off, I went to the Players Club in Philadelphia where actors would hang out. There I met two wonderful players: Jean Simmons (even more beautiful in person) and Margaret Hamilton who in 1939 had played the unforgettable witch in *The Wizard of Oz*. They were starring in the Broadway bound Sondheim musical, *A Little Night Music*. We sat together and I confessed to Margaret Hamilton how I had been so terrified of her witch in the Oz film that I had started screaming so loudly that the manager had made us leave the theatre. She then shared with me that playing that role almost destroyed her career. "For years, no one could picture me as anything but the witch!"

The atmosphere in rehearsals was somewhat difficult. By now, Martin Balsam, our Willy Loman, was being openly abused by our volatile director. Anti-Semitic and wanting the role for himself, George C. Scott was making Balsam's life a pure misery. Scott travelled with a bodyguard — not to protect him but to make sure he didn't get drunk and start a fight which he was prone to do. Working with Scott was like daily being near a time bomb and not knowing when it might explode. The

atmosphere was unhealthy for all of us. One night I spotted Marty, alone in the hotel bar with his head hung low. I sat down next to him, not sure of what to say.

"I'm thinking of quitting, Catherine. I can't take much of this anymore."

"Marty, you're the star of this show. Tell the producer that either Scott goes or you do."

He did and George was gone the next day. We had ten more days of rehearsal and wondered who would direct? Well, none other than the playwright himself!

I was 34 and Arthur, 62. He seemed drawn to me and I guessed that this was a pattern with the famous playwright and younger actresses. I knew he was married and for me, that meant off limits. I could not betray another woman. And I was still faithful to my husband. He accepted this and we spent time together as friends — not lovers. Other members of the cast would see us walking late at night, having dinner, and then breakfast the next morning, so they began to assume what, in fact, was not happening. One late night, in a coffee shop eating apple pie, Arthur said with humor, "Substituting apple pie instead of sex." Arthur had just returned from the Beijing production of *Death of a Salesman* and was amazed how well it had been received. Two years later, I would understand why it was so well received when my first full-length play, *On the*

Edge: The Final Years of Virginia Woolf, was translated and published in Beijing. When I met the Chinese poet who had translated my play and who had survived years of abuse during Mao's Cultural Revolution, I asked him why the Chinese would be interested in Virginia Woolf. He replied, "Because she committed suicide." As did Willy Loman in *Salesman.*

During our Philadelphia days together, I mentioned that I was psychic and could read ordinary playing cards. Arthur asked me to read for him so I went to his room and proceeded to do so. I knew no details about his current wife, Inge Morath, but during the reading commented that she was depressed and had some mental imbalance. Later he shared that it was a residue of

Arthur Miller (1915-2005)

the holocaust. Miller also spoke of the McCarthy period where so many had been blacklisted due to Communist sympathizing. It struck me that he spoke of it as though it had just occurred last week and not several years before. He spoke about his marriage to Marilyn Monroe and how he had to leave the marriage for his own survival, and that "no one could have saved Marilyn".

Later when I returned to New York, I ran into an actor friend of mine on the street who exclaimed, "Hi, I heard you had an affair with Arthur Miller!" I told him truthfully that it was not so, but wasn't sure he believed me. A few days later, I received in the mail, a copy of a book of short stories by Arthur Miller who had signed the book, "with gratitude". The book's title told me something as well: *I Don't Need You Anymore.*

I visited him once in his NY apartment where he showed me a table and chair that he had designed and built. The craftmanship was flawless — as were his plays. As I was beginning to write the Virginia Woolf play, *On the Edge,* I asked him how many drafts of *Salesman* he had written. He thought for a moment then said, "Thirty-six." I was beginning to learn a valuable lesson: writing is re-writing.

A few weeks later, I was cast as Patsy Jefferson in *The Patriots,* a bio-play of Thomas Jefferson and his daughter, Patsy, by Pulitzer Prize-winning playwright, Sidney Kingsley. Our rehearsals were at the Asolo Theatre in an eighteenth-century theatre the Ringling Brothers had purchased and brought over piece by piece from Italy to Sarasota, Florida.

It was winter and our NY cast was thrilled to be in sunny Florida. I was given an apartment on the lagoon leading to the ocean. I would sit outside sunning, learning my lines, and watching dolphins dive and play. It was lovely. The audience was too large for the small theatre so we performed the show in 'the purple monster'— as we called it — a gigantic theatre in downtown Sarasota.

After we opened the show, we were given a day off. The cast wanted to drive to a nearby city to see a play. I opted to be dropped off at the Everglades National Park to hike on my own. Told to watch out for crocodiles, I was left and a new adventure began. After walking for some time, I saw a solitary tree without leaves amidst the flat everglades, and climbed it, then had my lunch of dried nuts and fruits. The sun was quite hot so I lay back on a branch and took a nap. After sometime, I opened my eyes and noticed large vultures circling high above me. I closed my eyes again and a few minutes later opened my eyes and saw the vultures diving only a few feet from me, getting closer all the time. Shocked into action, I began waving my arms and shouting, "I'm alive! I'm alive!" I had been still for so long that they must have thought I was dead prey.

Patsy Jefferson in *The Patriots* with Robert Murch, 1976

Luckily, *The Patriots* received excellent reviews and we were chosen for a *Great Performances* television production of the play for PBS national television. The crew came down from NY to Florida so we were able to stay in the sun for another six weeks and film there. Jac Venza, our executive producer, had garnered more Emmy nominations than anyone. Later back in NY, we were all invited to the Pulitzer playwright Sidney Kingsley's sprawling flat in Soho to watch the show air on television. It was such a pleasure to meet Kingsley and his lovely actress wife, Madge Evans, the original Patsy Jefferson, who liked my performance..

During the run of *The Patriots*, I had made the decision to quit acting. Outwardly, it made little sense as my career as an actor was doing well — especially after playing the female lead on national television. Unexpectedly, the desire to perform simply fell away as naturally as an autumn leaf. All in all, I had acted in fifty-five plays, and in all but two, had played leading roles. Three months after this decision, I realized that the acting years had planted the seed for a new career as a playwright.

Often when I am teaching workshops or speaking at conferences, I am asked how I find the discipline to write. I often reply with this true story about a fine painter who taught me what discipline is. When I first arrived in New York City, a young and fledgling actress in my twenties, I met the author, Gerald Sykes, and his artist wife, Buffy Johnson. One afternoon, Buffy invited me to her studio. I was amazed at her oil paintings, similar to those of Georgia O'Keeffe — only far more intricate. One painting would take months to complete. I remarked on her great discipline to do such work. Still painting, she sternly remarked, "Don't you know? Discipline is love." Buffy Johnson is gone now but not the lesson she taught me. Or her splendid paintings that live on in the Metropolitan Museum of Art in New York City. Hers was a labor of love — not discipline. And yet, I have yet to discover a better definition of discipline than hers.

> The more you are motivated by love,
> the more fearless and free your action will be.
>
> Dalai Lama

One evening, after returning from my annual trip to India, I attended a party given by Gerald Sykes and Buffy Johnson. As soon as I entered their home, Gerald said, "You must meet someone who also loves India." He brought me to a tall, athletic, engaging Joseph Campbell. Gerald introduced us by saying that I had just returned from India. Joe responded, saying that India had changed his life due to meeting a great sage there. When I asked who the sage was, Joe replied, "Oh, you wouldn't know him. He refused to be a public figure like most today." I persisted and finally Joe revealed his name. I waited before replying then said softly, "I have just returned from his son who is my Teacher." Surprised and moved, Joe took my hand then pulled me across the room to a quiet corner where we sat and talked for half an hour. Here a friendship began. I'm always struck that when the focus is on the spiritual, how Spirit guides us wisely and we meet those we are meant to meet. Joe introduced me to his talented wife, Jean Erdman, dancer/choreographer, and her wonderful theatre, The Open Eye, where she often directed plays by W.B. Yeats.

Sometimes Joe and I would see off-Broadway plays together. Once we saw a rather mediocre play and went out afterwards. Joe spoke eloquently comparing the play to 5th century Greek drama and the current war in Viet Nam. His expansive mind knew no limits. At one point, I laughed, saying, "Joe, this conversation is ten times more interesting than the play we just saw!" What remains with me to this day is something Joe had that few retain in their professional lives: an undying boyish enthusiasm for his work. In Joe's case, that work was the study of archetypal mythology. All too often we begin with enthusiasm yet as professionals, the years sometimes dampen it. Not with Joe. And his enthusiasm was contagious. What a gift he was to his students — and friends!

We must be willing to let go of the life

we planned

So as to have the life that is waiting for us.

Joseph Campbell

1904-1987

Another great friend and godfather to my son was Robert Payne, author of a hundred and ten books — both fiction and non-

Robert Payne (12/4/11-3/3/83)

fiction. Payne was known for his best-selling biographies as well. Born in Cornwall, England, he always seemed to be in the right place at the right time.

Payne was cultural attaché for the British Embassy in Beijing from 1941-1946. In 1946, Payne met and interviewed Mao Zedong, providing background for his 1950 biography, *Mao Tze-tung: Ruler of Red China.* During this interview, Mao correctly predicted that it would take only a year and half for the Communist forces to conquer China. Payne had married Rose, a Chinese princess, who refused to leave China when Payne had no choice except to return to England due to the increasing conflict caused by the Communist revolution. Though they never met again, Payne continued to support her. Later he met Adolf Hitler in Germany before England entered the war. In Hollywood, he met Charlie Chaplin and Greta Garbo, later writing biographies of all these, and many other major personalities of the times.

During the years I worked as an actor, I would often call Robert for research information on a role I was to audition for or for one I had been cast to play. More often than not, he had written a book about the history of that period. Like Joseph Campbell, Robert remained in love with writing and with those creative individuals he knew and wrote about.

Once, he invited me to a small party at his home on

Central Park West in honor of the legendary French mime, Marcel Marceau, currently performing on Broadway in his one-man show. At one point, in my friend's living room overlooking Central Park, Marceau stood up and spontaneously began to perform his famous mime of catching a butterfly — without make-up or costume. I was spellbound, realizing that without the traditional white face of a clown, it was all the more poignant. Naked. Vulnerable. Simplicity was the key. Then a kind of epiphany occurred with crystal clarity. This was not about a man chasing a butterfly, but human beings trying to capture Life — and how vulnerable we all are in this persistent pursuit.

> Do not the most moving moments of our lives
> find us all without words?
>
> Marcel Marceau

Unfortunately, Robert was unlucky in love and though I could not respond to his romantic feelings for me, we maintained a close friendship. When he finally found a bride, a woman from north India, I was his 'best man' at the wedding at St. John the Divine, making sure he looked nice and that the ring was not lost. The marriage was a grave mistake and before long, Robert knew it. We had lost touch as his new wife had insisted that he not see me though we were nothing more than friends. One morning he called and asked me to meet him for a drink at the

Algonquin Hotel, a favorite hangout for authors since the 1920s renown Round Table with the likes of Dorothy Parker, George S. Kaufman, Harpo Marx, and many others. Robert told me, "She won't allow me to see you. It doesn't make sense as you were my friend long before she appeared." I could tell he was unhappy, and I was probably little comfort. What could one say?

Though I did not know then, it would be the last time I would see my friend. Soon after, his wife insisted they take a Caribbean holiday and demanded that he leave his typewriter behind. Now everyone who knew Robert Payne knew that Robert wrote every single day, usually from 12 am to 6 am, as there were no disturbances during these hours. And that he lived to write. I learned a few days later that on the second night of their holiday, after a quarrel with his new wife, Robert had a stroke or heart attack and died in the Men's Room in some fancy restaurant. His longtime agent for decades and friend, Bertha Klausner, was fired by Robert's widow. As Bertha told me later, "We had no contracts, you see. It was all based on friendship and trust." The wife got greedy, and as there were royalties coming in from over 110 books, why share with an agent? The memorial was at Columbia University and many came. I sat at the back and did not attend the reception afterwards. Robert Payne was only seventy-two. His own father had lived well into his nineties. What a loss — both personally and collectively.

There were, of course, rejections, near misses, as is the actor's lot. I was considered for the role of Ramola, the wife of Nijinsky played years later by Nureyev in the film, *Nijinsky*. The film producer arranged for me to meet Nureyev backstage when he was removing his ballet shoes after a performance. I could not take my eyes off his feet which reminded me of the larger than life hand of Michelangelo's *David*. The feet were larger than life, all muscle — even distorted as most professional dancers are. The film was delayed for some years but eventually made with Nureyev — without me.

I was called back and screen tested for the role of Elaine Robinson in *The Graduate with* Dustin Hoffman, but Katharine Ross got the part. They decided I did not look American enough. Perhaps those years in India wearing a sari? Or because I was using my married name, Katherine Rao. Pity. What a privilege it would have been to be directed by Mike Nichols.

Then the role of St. Clare in Zeffirelli's *Brother Sun, Sister Moon.* They practically decided on an English cast closer to Italy where they shot this lovely film about St. Francis.

And Coppola's amazing *The Godfather* when I was called back and screen tested for the role of Al Pacino's first wife who was blown up in a car explosion. They sensibly cast a local Italian actress as the film was shot there. This is just to illustrate how rejection is so much a part of being an actor. My friend, Jill Andre who had played my aunt in Albee's *A Delicate Balance* in Cincinnati was on Broadway in a new play with John Cullum, *The Trip Back Down,* and had invited me to see the show then have supper with Cullum and herself. The play only ran a few days, but I remember one great line. It's about a racing car driver from a midwestern town who was a champion but in later years begins to lose the races. He returns home for a visit and someone taunts him for losing the race. He turns and looks at a man who has never left their hometown and says, "Just remember, in order to lose, you have to be in the race." Great line and one I often quote to my students and consultant clients.

Young Christopher, ten, was now living with my mother and step-father. I really missed my son. Nightly phone calls, stolen weekends, holidays and summers were not enough. I decided to bring him to New York — not for a visit this time, but for always. I could no longer bear the separations.

I had been cast in a daytime television series called *Love of Life*, then the longest running daytime drama. I played Erica Birney, a nurse in love with a handsome doctor. Unfortunately, he was in love with the blonde bitch, so for a year and a half, I mooned and brooded. The fortunate thing, other than a good salary, was that I could walk to the CBS Studio from Lincoln Towers where we lived, at 7:30am five days a week and be home by 3:30, about the time my son returned from Elementary School, one short block from our apartment. Beginning the sixth grade in NY, Christopher was so happy as was I.

Through a lawyer friend, I learned of Hunter College High School, a special school supported by the City for bright students. I recalled what we had been told in Austin of the need to find a suitable school for this precocious child. It worked like this. Each elementary school in NYC would choose one student to compete for entrance to Hunter by taking a three-hour exam.

Christopher, 12, Catherine, 32, NY

Christopher was chosen by his school to compete. The top two hundred students who scored the highest marks were then chosen to enter the seventh grade at Hunter and remain through the 12th grade. Not surprisingly, Christopher won his place. This was good for another reason: our son did not stick out as the odd one now because all the other students at Hunter were as bright as he was. Cynthia Nixon (*Sex and the City*) and Lin-Manuel Miranda (*Hamilton* the Musical) are just two of Hunter's remarkable graduates. Though he was offered scholarships at prestigious private schools, like Trinity and Collegiate, he decisively stated he would not wear a uniform, and too, I rather liked the idea that the Hunter students were chosen for their merit and not their parents' wealth.

We were still sharing a studio apartment with one bathroom on the 25th floor in Lincoln Towers when I first heard of Manhattan Plaza — later called 'the miracle on 43rd Street'.

Manhattan Plaza was originally built for the wealthy. Two tower buildings, forty stories each, and on the Plaza or second level it had an urban park with trees, basketball courts, racquet ball courts, and an enormous swimming pool covered by a glass ceiling that opened to the sky when the weather was sunny. The location was 400 W. 43rd St and Ninth Avenue—two blocks from Times Square. What the real estate developers did not bank on was that the wealthy did not wish to live one block from the pornographic movie theatres and the busy trade of hookers prowling Ninth Avenue, and only two blocks from Times Square. So, this posh apartment complex became a white elephant. That is, until H.U.D. stepped in and took it over as subsidized living for professional 'union-carrying card members' of the performing arts. With Christopher, eleven, now living full time with me in New York, the studio apartment was no longer an option. I hesitated due to the location so near an unsavory atmosphere. Christopher, more practical than his mother, cleverly advised, "Mother, go ahead and fill out the forms. We can always say 'no' later."

And so it was, thanks to being a member of Actors Equity, SAG, and AFTRA that on the second day the building opened, we moved into a spacious 2 BR, 2 Bath apartment on the thirty-seventh floor with a terrace. The view from all the rooms was of the Hudson River and luxury liners entering and leaving, the Empire State Building, and the World Trade Towers. The population of the two tower buildings of Manhattan Plaza was over four thousand. The miracle was that within a year, the prostitutes and drug dealers had moved elsewhere. The street across on 43rd Street was converted into several off-Broadway theatres with trees planted in front of each building. Restaurants such as 'Curtain Up' on the first floor of our building and other artsy cafes popped up overnight. After years of trying to clean up the Times Square area, H.U.D. had triumphed. In this case, our government did something right! There was a population explosion during our first two years, as acting couples could now afford to have children!

It worked like this. When an actor was working, we paid regular market value rent. When we were not working, the rent dropped to an unbelievable low. Each year we had to submit copies of our IRS statement to keep us honest.

> Writing is my vacation from living.
> Eugene O'Neill

One of the two plays I had written in college, was produced off-Broadway at the Cubiculo Theatre in the early seventies. *Somewhere-in-Between* is set in an insane asylum and the theme, as said by Ben who feigns insanity in order to return to the asylum, "The truth is that out there, they are more insane than we are in here." The play received an excellent review in the *NY TIMES* where the critic spoke of the obvious influence on the playwright of the popular author and Scottish psychiatrist, R.D. Laing (*The Divided Self*). The fact was I had never read or even heard of R.D. Laing, so I remarked in jest to a friend, "I had better go buy his book to see how he influenced me!" Critics.

Another interesting, if unexpected, situation occurred during the run of this play.

A woman I had never met asked to meet the playwright afterwards then proceeded to talk to me as though I were a psychiatrist. I tried repeatedly to excuse myself, saying that I was only a playwright — not a doctor. Well, that poor woman followed me for three blocks, convinced that I could help her with her mental problems! I marvel that some people assume when one succeeds in one area that they are also experts in other unrelated fields!

Because of Manhattan Plaza and Christopher being accepted into Hunter College High School, I could afford to stop acting and be a full-time mother, and devote myself to a new career as a playwright. I had recently acted in an off-Broadway comedy about the English author, Virginia Woolf and Bloomsbury. Preparing for the role, I had read all of Woolf's novels as well as the splendid biography by Quentin Bell. Good notices in the *NY Times* praising my performance as Woolf, said, "And she even looks like Virginia Woolf!" After the play's run, I was still reading about Woolf. Then for the next three weeks, I sat down daily at my electric typewriter in the corner of my bedroom overlooking the Hudson River and wrote my first long play: *On the Edge: The Final Years of Virginia Woolf.* The play won a National Endowment for the Arts award which provided funding to live on for one whole year. So, the dye was cast. No more auditions. No more acting (or so I thought then).

On the Edge: The Final Years of Virginia Woolf (Originally titled *Virginia)* was set during WW II in England. The play explores a woman's struggle with madness in a world gone mad

Virginia and Leonard Woolf

with war. The play was chosen to have its first outing at the Aspen Playwrights Festival in Aspen, Colorado. And theatre legend Harold Clurman was assigned to direct the first production. He and the New York cast were transplanted to Aspen, along with the playwright. The 1978 production was well received. In one speech, I had Virginia Woolf's husband, Leonard, describe what had happened in Germany on Kristallnacht or the 'Night of Broken Glass' in 1938 — called that because of all the synagogues and Jewish businesses that were destroyed. That night began the pogrom against the Jews throughout Nazi Germany, becoming a preview of the horrors to come. After one performance, an older woman I did not know, came up to thank me for including this part of history. Tightly holding my hand and almost sobbing, she said, "I was there. I was there."

Somehow the well-known actress, Kim Stanley, had heard about the play and called me to say she had always wanted to play Virginia Woolf. Might she read my play? She gave me her address and a time to bring the play to her. I rang her bell and a voice on the other side of the door, said, "Just leave the script on the doorstep." Disappointed not to see her in person, I did as she said. Only later did I understand why. Stanley who had played *The* Goddess (Hollywood) was now living as a recluse, an alcoholic, hugely overweight, and must have known that she could not physically play the part. Sad. Such a great talent. After returning home, I imagined Kim Stanley sitting alone in her apartment reading my play out loud, and probably reading it brilliantly.

Later, I sent the play to Jose Quintero whom I had met when we almost worked together in the play, *Gandhi*. Quintero loved the play and found a Broadway producer, Eliot Martin, and began to work with me on some rewrites. We each wanted Vanessa Redgrave to play the lead and she accepted. The two weeks working with Quintero were a great education. He asked me to read Virginia while he read aloud all the other roles and suggested changes — most of which I heartily accepted. I was in Texas briefly and when I returned to NY, I learned the sad news. Vanessa Redgrave, a political activist, was rallying media attention with her pro-Palestinian movement. At this time, all the Broadway theatres were owned by the Shuberts and other Jewish producers, and they boycotted Redgrave from Broadway. So here politics intruded on art. I have always regretted this as Redgrave was totally perfect for the role and the right age to play Virginia Woolf. That's show biz. One has no choice but to move on. *On the Edge* would later be seen at the Long Wharf Theatre in New Haven, Connecticut and other regional theatres, with exceptional responses.

When I received the National Endowment for the Arts grant for my first full-length play, *On the Edge,* the grant winners were asked to write a response. I wrote that apart from the support and encouragement, the money to live for one year provides time without pressure.

Encouraged by the response, I committed to writing eleven other plays over the next few years. This would require allies. I owe a debt to several art colonies and the essential service they provide to artists. When I stopped acting to pursue playwriting, I began to spend one month each year at Yaddo, MacDowell Colony, Ossabaw, or Edna St. Vincent Millay

Retreat. There I would write a first draft of a new play. My good friend, Robert, a buddy from Austin, would fly up from Texas and stay with my teenage son. It worked out beautifully for all as Robert, an excellent astrologer, began to get NY clients, my son had a guy to stay with, and I had time and solitude to write

Catherine in NY, 1978

first drafts of the plays.

Once my plays began receiving productions and awards, I was asked to teach playwriting at The New School University. When first invited, I said to the Dean, "Writing can't be taught." Then he replied, "Then teach it from that perspective." I was so taken with the Dean's answer that I was hooked, teaching there for the next eight years. I called the class, "The Writing On-Your-Feet Playwriting Workshop" where I incorporated improvisations and acting exercises to illustrate that dramatic writing is not to be read but seen and heard. I later heard from others that The New School was unique in that it sought teachers who actually *did* and succeeded in whatever they were teaching. Graduate degrees meant less than actual professional experience. Smart.

After the first year, I added another course, *Lives in the Theatre* where I interviewed actors, playwrights, and producers who worked in the theatre. After interviewing the guest for one hour, I would open to Q and A with the audience and they could ask whatever they wanted. It was a popular course and never dull as most of the NY audience were seasoned theatre goers. One actor was Jason Robards who spoke of his recovery from alcoholism after a near fatal car accident. His son, Sam, also an actor, was in the audience, and I felt Jason was speaking mostly to his son that evening. (A few years later, Jason Robards would star with Julie Harris in my first screenplay, *The Christmas Wife* (HBO).

During the eight years teaching graduate school, I had the wonderful habit of dropping by the Strand Used Bookstore in Greenwich Village only a few blocks from the university. One day, I happened upon a collection of letters written by Calamity

Jane to her daughter, Wild Bill Hickok being the father. Lightning struck and I had found my next play: *Calamity Jane,* a legend in her own time who lived a century too early as the strong willed, liberated woman she was. Forced to give up her daughter, Janey, for adoption when Wild Bill Hickok leaves her for another woman, the story explores the confrontation between mother and daughter as well as the myth and reality of the Old West. (This true story is a far cry from the Doris Day film.)

Invited to Ossabaw Island, one of four writers given lodging, food, time and space to write, I flew to Savannah, Georgia while Robert stayed with Christopher, who was sixteen now. There on Ossabaw, a privately-owned island the size of Manhattan, I wrote *Calamity Jane.* It could not have been more perfect. An isolated island only a short ferry ride from Savannah, no cars, deserted beach, untamed country with wild boars, donkeys, horses, and alligators. The only law was a resident Sheriff with a holstered pistol, looking more like a cowboy than a modern-day sheriff. It was not difficult to imagine the Wild West there!

Calamity Jane has had several productions in and out of New York, and later I wrote the book for the musical adaptation which has had several productions as well.

The first production was in Albany, NY before an audience of 1200 or more. My mother and son came to see the premiere. I remember vomiting in the hotel bathroom just before leaving for the theatre. After years acting in plays, I was at a loss — experiencing that the only one who has absolutely nothing to do on Opening Night is the playwright! Luckily, the show went well and had such a huge response that the following year the same theatre revived the production.

***Calamity Jane* (1852-1903)**

Though optioned for Broadway along with two other of my produced plays (*On the Edge* and *The Women of Cedar Creek)* none would tread the Great White Way. I sadly realized that *Calamity Jane* as my other work were American Plays if not Broadway ones. That's show biz, too. But happily, each of the eleven plays have had a life outside NY.

With every play, I creatively began to form myself from the inside out, with inspiration arising unexpectedly from unusual places.

Walking along Park Avenue one afternoon, I spied a headline in the *New York Post* about a woman who had jumped out of an upper story brownstone with her small child. Intuitively, I knew this would be my next play. I purposefully refrained from reading the article as the headline was enough to ignite the play. Written about the time my marriage ended, I wrote a line the heroine says, "If I had stayed nineteen forever, we'd still be happily married. But I grew up." I later called this my angry woman play while others labeled it a feminist play. It is about the pressures on a young woman in the 1980s to be super woman: a perfect wife and mother with a successful career. What happens when her husband is unfaithful and she goes over the edge? The play explores the myths projected on men and women that, in the end, imprison them.

The play was produced one evening at The Actors Studio

in NY where I was a member of the Playwrights/Directors Unit. I cast and directed the play. Famed director Arthur Penn (*Bonnie and Clyde*) would moderate a Q and A with the audience following the end of the show. I was nervous as at this time, the subject of a mother killing her own child had not yet been seen — at least not since *Medea* in 5th century Greece. At the end of the play, Arthur Penn, said to all there, "I hate this play. Furthermore, no mother would do such a thing." Stunned as a moderator is supposed to be neutral, I didn't know how to respond. Suddenly a woman from the audience loudly spoke, "Oh, yes she would. And if not, she would certainly consider it!" Then another woman piped up and agreed. Afterwards, novelist Norman Mailer approached to say how much he loved the play. He said that at the end of Act II, the hair at the back of his neck stood up, and he felt in the presence of a genuine American tragedy. Well, this remark from such a great novelist certainly took the sting out of director Arthur Penn's response!

Later when I began writing films in Hollywood, I pitched *The Myth of Annie Beckman* as a possible movie to a studio. It was the late eighties and the studio said that no one wants to see a movie about this. I told them that within three years, a film about this subject would be seen. And exactly three years later, a television movie was made starring Farrah Fawcett (*Charlie's Angels*), based on a true story of a Texas woman drowning her children. Creatives often manifest ideas too soon. "Timing is all" as Shakespeare said.

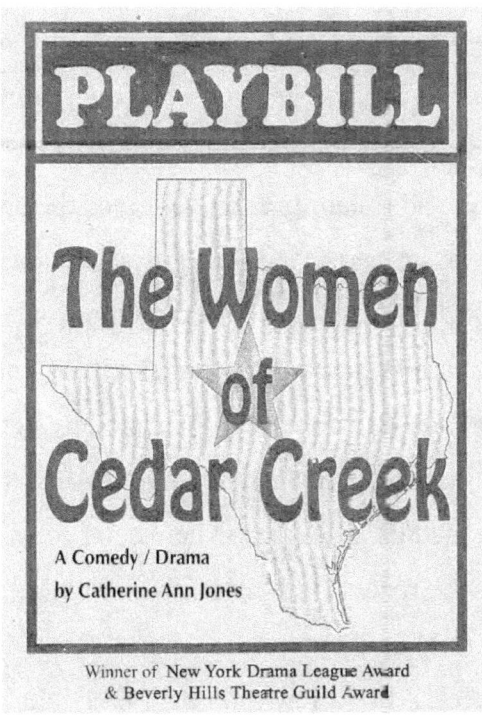

I grew up in New Orleans (and Texas from age seven) listening to women's stories. My grandmother would have her friends over for a quilting bee. They would sit in a wide circle and work on the same quilt, sewing bits and pieces of material into one enduring whole. At the same time, the women would share bits and pieces of their lives with one another which made of their friendships another kind of quilt. I can remember even now myself at the age of five or six sitting on the staircase just around the corner, unseen, mesmerized by these vibrant Southern voices. Eventually, all this led to the all-female character play, *The Women of Cedar Creek*.

These works, cut from our own past, are sometimes the toughest to write because to write our own stories brings up ghosts and long buried emotions. In writing my early plays about Virginia Woolf and Calamity Jane, I avoided the one play I knew I had one day to write: the inevitable dysfunctional family play every playwright must face. After seeing four of my plays produced, the family play began to make itself known, a gentle tapping at my chamber door. Still I resisted by not sitting down to write the play. However, I did begin to save scraps of dialogue and character details. Out of nowhere, bits of dialogue would pop up out of the recesses of my mind and I would dutifully jot them down, tossing them into a shoebox in my New York apartment closet. After a few months, I had quite a pile. Then I was invited to Yaddo, the Art Colony in Saratoga Springs, New York, to write. At Yaddo, I felt the ghosts of those who had come before: Katherine Ann Porter, Carson McCullers, John Cheever, and so many fine writers.

It was clear that I could not put this play off any longer though the inner child was still reluctant to tackle those early Texas years. I created a process which I have never used with any other project. (Often each project requires its own process.)

At Yaddo, I asked for a large bulletin board and tacks. Then at the top of the board I tacked slips of paper with the name of six characters and under each character's name, I pinned the collected shoebox scraps of dialogue. Pretty soon, I had a board covered with dialogue and six characters in search of an author. I always felt I made this play as my grandmother had made her quilts: saving scraps of material and later arranging these scraps of the past together into a work of art.

I knew that *The Women of Cedar Creek* was a story which had to come out, for therapeutic reasons, if not for the sake of art. I had no illusions about selling this one. I simply had to get it out of my system. During my Yaddo stay, I wrote a very specific play about growing up in Texas and being formed by powerful Southern women who were at war with themselves and each other. At the end, it was as if a ghost had been exorcised. I was free of the past and could move on.

Imagine my surprise when that play went on to win the New York Drama League Award and the Beverly Hills Theatre Guild Award! People would see the play and say, "I'm from Kansas, and that's my family exactly. How could you know?" Or someone from Toronto would exclaim, "That's my mother" or "That's my sister. How could you know?"

In this way, I learned from this experience to tell my students that the universal is carried by a specific place and specific characters. Anton Chekov was a master of the specific. He wrote about provincial Russian people he knew and his themes and characters are as universally true today as when they were written well over a century ago.

Never forget that the best tools you have as a writer are yourself, your memories, your values, your point of view or life perspective, your doubts, fears, and obsessions. Especially your doubts, fears, and obsessions. Dare to be personal! This alone makes your story unique. Write from yourself, not from what you think the market dictates. Such stories take tremendous courage as they arise from your very own wounded soul. These stories will carry the power of the gods and result in universal, archetypal myths. Please understand that I am not advocating to necessarily, literally write your own life story — though you may wish to do so. Rather, I am encouraging you to tap into your feelings about your own memories and imbue those passions and fears and sorrows into your fictional or non-fictional story. Invest your own feelings, fears, and conflicts in order to birth an authentic story. Be emotionally autobiographical.

Please note that the Texas play was not a literal representation of my family of origin, but I used place and real prototypes to make the play real, first to me and then later to an audience.

Whatever our theme in writing, it is old and
tried.
It is only the vision that can be new, but that
is enough.

Eudora Welty

The idea that fascinated me was that a family can say and do terrible things to each other and usually do, yet, at the end of the day, sit down and eat chicken together as though nothing were out of the ordinary. I borrowed from Aristotle the classic unities of time, space, and theme, and was on my way. That is, the play took place in one setting, one twenty-four-hour period, and was about one theme: the destructive and unifying bond of family.

I had applied for a Fulbright Research Grant for India and to my surprise, was chosen. I began to prepare for a year studying early pre-Hindu shamanic forms of ritual, dance, and storytelling in south India. Weary of the commercial pressures of Broadway, I wanted to explore storytelling in cultures that carried a deeper meaning. I, also, of course, wanted an excuse to spend more time with my Teacher. I took my son out of school with his commitment to keep a journal of his experience, and to keep up his school work.

After an amazing year in India where apart from obtaining video tapes of soon to be extinct shamanic rituals and early dance forms, I wrote a play, *The Hill*, for ages twelve and up. It was translated into Malayalam and produced by a well-known director in Kerala. I also taught acting at the National School of Drama in New Delhi. Using inner methods to create a role became a revolutionary act among the staff — though the students responded enthusiastically. During a performance as I was going to my seat in the audience, one of the student actors came up the aisle and prostrated at my feet. Though embarrassed, I understood why he was grateful. Until now, they had been taught only external disciplines (voice and body) and not encouraged or taught how to bring themselves and their own emotional history to the role.

After India, I returned to Yaddo in upstate New York. There I would sit daily, writing my first screenplay, *The Christmas Wife.*

Soon after writing a first draft of the screenplay, I received an invitation to fly to Hollywood as *The Women of Cedar Creek* play had just been awarded the Beverly Hills Theatre Guild Award. My family knew nothing of this play, though fictional, it dealt with certain family secrets such as my mother's alcoholism. So, I had not mentioned the play to my mother due to its contents, but when she read in the newspapers about the awards, she asked me about it. She also said she wanted to come with me to Hollywood to see me receive the award and to watch a production of the play. I told her she'd better read the play first and then decide. After posting her a copy of the inevitable dysfunctional family play, I heard nothing. Finally, I braced myself and called, asking if she had read the play. Long pause. Then "Yes". I asked her if she still wanted to come to Hollywood with me. Another long pause. Then "Yes, only don't tell anyone who's who." I laughed, saying, "It's a deal." So, we flew to Los Angeles and were put up in the Roosevelt Hotel in Hollywood.

Writing *The Christmas Wife*

I was first to attend a banquet in Beverly Hills, receive a generous check and award presented by theatre legend Julie Harris, then attend the first production of *The Women of Cedar Creek*. At the last minute while packing, I had tossed in a draft of the recently completed screenplay, *The Christmas Wife*. Unknown to me, another fork in the road was looming as soon MGM would option *The Women of Cedar Creek* for a film.

Mother thoroughly enjoyed the Beverly Hills banquet and meeting recognizable movie stars. That same evening, we went to the theatre to see the first outing of the play. I had kept my word and not divulged to anyone the identity of the prototypes. However, just before the play began, Mother tapped my actress friend, Jillian, on the shoulder and whispered, "I'm Bobbie!" Goes to show that no matter what you say about them, everyone wants to be immortalized!

When I had returned from the Fulbright year in India, I had caught a cold or flu on the airline and arrived exhausted and unwell. I had allowed a student from my class at The New School to stay in the apartment though we were not allowed to sublet. I returned to discover the lock changed on the door so could not enter. She told me through the door that she and a friend of hers had taken over the apartment. It is commonly known that people will kill to get a good apartment in NY! Shocked at the betrayal, I went downstairs to the lobby and was standing there not knowing what to do, when Victor Stoloff, a gentleman I had briefly met earlier approached. He and his wife lived on the 40th floor in my building. Finding me in tears, he asked, "What's wrong?" I told him. He smiled and said, "We are leaving tonight for Europe, you can stay in our flat." Angel on my shoulder! So, I stayed there and sorted the dilemma. I later discovered that this treacherous and not quite stable student had used my address book and looked up my friends to meet them and learn more about me. She even went to Austin to take a course at the University where I had schooled. Little by little, she was trying to become me. Weird. I went to the office the next day, confessed that I had let someone stay in the apartment and would be giving it up. I also made sure that the culprits did not keep the 37th floor apartment. With my son away at university and an offer to teach for a year at the same university where he was, I decided to leave NY. For the past three years, I had felt that it was time to leave NY but wanted to wait until Christopher graduated high school. It had now been a year away in India and I had not made plans to leave — until now. Were it not for the student who tried to steal my apartment, I might not have left at all. C.G. Jung once said that when you don't heed subtle messages, something may come and hit you over the head. I guess I needed the nudge. Amazing how a negative event sometimes becomes a positive one in disguise!

The University of Texas offer to teach came with a generous salary. Three departments joined to bring me to Austin: The Asian Department where I would offer an Introductory course on the culture and philosophy of India, and the English and Drama Departments where I would teach graduate play-writing.

With Christopher, now a sophomore at UT-Austin, we set up home in a duplex in front of the garage apartment that was our first home in Austin. I had brought our NY cat, Sebastian, so now a family of three, Austin became our new home. This experience becoming college roommates with my son had its ups and downs, and later led to a comedy screenplay I would write for Universal Studios. (See Part V: Hollywood)

With *The Women of Cedar Creek* optioned by MGM and interest in my first screenplay, *The Christmas Wife,* I was ready, after teaching in Austin, to take the plunge and go west to the City of Angels.

> To write is to create a space
> in which things can happen.
> To live one's life the same.
>
> Michael Adam, *Man is a Little World*

Part V Touched by Angels
Hollywood, 1988-1993

All things create themselves from

their own innermost reflection and

none can tell how they came to do so.

Chuang Tzu

With John and Jillian in Hollywood

Change is the very movement of life. Yet it is also all too often the factor we most resist. To resist change is to resist life itself. Before the great exodus to Hollywood and after teaching in Austin, Texas, I returned to NY to pack and officially give up the wonderful 37th floor apartment at Manhattan Plaza, our home for ten years. I sold or gave away almost everything except several boxes of books and my Scandinavian backless typing chair (which incidentally, I still have). And two suitcases of clothes. I told The New School that I would not be teaching there the following term, and said my goodbyes to friends.

My friend from college days, Jillian Lindig and her husband, John Michalski, had moved to Hollywood for acting work before I moved west, and found an apartment for me in the building next door to them. It is no small thing to have friends in Los Angeles. They later moved back to New York though happily, the friendship continues.

Stoloff, my kind angel, who had lent me his apartment in Manhattan Plaza, suggested I contact Edie Landau, a producer in Hollywood. I had not realized before that Victor Stoloff had himself been a producer and responsible for the hit television series, *Hawaii Five O*. Apart from Jillian and her husband, John — actors now living in Hollywood — the only person I knew was Julie Harris who had recently committed to playing the title role in *The Christmas Wife*. Before I left NY, I noticed that Jason Robards was starring in Eugene O'Neill's *The Iceman Cometh* in a splendid revival on Broadway, so with a copy of the screenplay in hand, I went to see the show. I had met Jason before during my acting years, and also when I interviewed him for my *Lives in the Theatre* class at The New School, so bracing myself, I ventured backstage. Fortunately, he remembered me. I told him that Julie Harris had already committed to *The Christmas Wife* and that he was my first choice for the male lead.

"You know, we had always wanted to work together but never have."

He took the script and called me the next day to say, "I'm in." I love NY actors! Coming from the theatre, they are real troupers. No star turns such as "Call my agent."

I knew almost no one in Hollywood except Julie Harris and soon I had two offers to produce *The Christmas Wife* along with two major stars attached. I never spoke to their agents nor discussed salaries. I remembered well-meaning friends telling me that I would never sell this script as it had no sex and no violence. Somehow, I knew — or hoped — that others like myself might want something different on television.

The first offer came from Network Television on the condition that I change the story. *The Christmas Wife* is a story about a senior recently widowed who, lonely, for the first time in his life rents a woman his own age to spend Christmas weekend with. The network executive first told me how much they loved my story then said, "What if when he rents the woman, instead of sixty-five, she's twenty-eight? Then 'what if 'when they go to the isolated cabin, a gang of rough kids break in and terrorize them? At first, I thought they were kidding, I laughed out loud then said, "Then it would be like any other television movie." Silence. They weren't kidding, so I said no. Then producer Edie Landau submitted the script to Colin Calendar at HBO. Fortunately, HBO liked the script as it was and produced it. HBO wanted Burt Lancaster for the male lead, but I insisted on Jason Robards as I felt he was better suited for this role. As a NY playwright who has control over casting, I assumed I did here. Of course, I later learned that Hollywood writers have no control whatsoever over script or casting. However, my innocence saved the day and HBO accepted Jason Robards. Sometimes it pays to be naïve.

As I had cast the two stars, I was given credit as associate producer. We shot in Toronto, Canada and I was invited to come, both as writer and producer. The thing was, that in both these capacities, my work had been done before getting on the plane. Consequently, except for a lovely lunch with the stars, Jason and Julie, I had nothing to do but stand around. Unlike stage rehearsals, watching a film shoot can be rather boring as mostly you wait quite a spell for the next shot which, when it finally comes, will be over in a few minutes. After one day of this, I gingerly asked if I might be excused. No problem. No script changes could be made at this late date due to rising costs, so on set, there is nothing more useless than the screenwriter.

Toronto, Canada is a wonderful place to shoot a film and

great crews, too. I took a day off to meet the now elderly Anna Mitchell-Hedges and see the Crystal Skull she discovered at age seventeen in an ancient Mayan dig in British Honduras (now Belize) in the 1920s. She left me alone with the skull and, overtaken with the strong psychic energy, I began to cry. Her life was amazing, a female Indiana Jones story. I asked for an option to write the film. She had already rejected several Hollywood offers, waiting for someone who could sense what the skull is. Fortunately for me, she felt I was the one. I wrote a treatment (long outline of the story) and tried to pitch the project to several studios to no avail. It was too early for this film. I moved on and was hired to write other movies, the first being a Hallmark Hall of Fame movie based on the bestselling novel, *Summertime.*

Julie Harris and Jason Robards on set for
The Christmas Wife

The Women of Cedar Creek play had earlier been optioned by MGM with an all-star cast. It was being packaged by legendary Lew Wasserman (Mr. Hollywood) of MCA who had gathered Julie Harris, Lee Remick, and Carol Burnett to star.

Alas, soon after, MGM went bankrupt so the film was never made. Another usual occurrence in Hollywood as I was to learn. This, too, is show biz!

Julie Harris became a good friend. After inviting Christopher and me to spend Christmas with her in Cape Cod where she lived, she invited me to stay in her second home in Brentwood as she would remain in Cape Cod, Massachusetts, for the summer.

Settled in Brentwood, one early morning I was suddenly awakened by the house shaking and the bedroom sliding glass door cracked a few feet from my bed. Being new to Los Angeles, my first thought when the bed shook was, "Oh, I didn't know there were subways in LA." This was my first but not last earthquake experience in California. The phone rang and I heard an unmistakable voice, "Julie? Julie? Are you all right?"

Is this Roddy McDowell?"

"Yes. Who are you?"

"My name is Catherine, a friend of Julie's. She's back in Cape Cod."

Though I had never before met Roddy McDowell, he had such a unique voice that I knew it was him. A wonderful actor since he was a child in many memorable movies such as *Lassie* and *How Green was My Valley*. I assume he and Julie became friends when they acted together in the adaptation of the Shirley Jackson thriller, *The Haunting* (1963). A couple of years later he would star with Dolly Parton in a movie I would write for Disney Studios called *Unlikely Angel*.

Thankfully, more screenwriting offers came my way, and as the sole paying parent, I was able to support most of the next four years of my son studies at The Kennedy School and Harvard Law School. Thank you, Hollywood!

The Christmas Wife aired on HBO, receiving over three hundred rave reviews, and was nominated for four Emmys including Best Film, Best Writing, Best Actor: Jason Robards. Best Actress: Julie Harris. At the ceremony which was nationally televised, they seated the nominees together on the first two rows. I was seated between two towering acting nominees, Christopher Reeves and Charlton Heston. I told my mother where to find me as she watched from Texas, "I'm seated between Superman and Moses!"

I soon became the flavor of the month for the next four years and was given much work writing television movies and feature films — a few were actually done. I was also invited by the Dean to teach graduate screenwriting at the Film School at USC (University of Southern California). When I told the Dean, a former New Yorker, I had only written one screenplay, she said she had admired my plays in New York and wanted screenwriting taught by someone with a background in play-writing. Unusual as well as propitious.

Amidst the hoopla surrounding *The Christmas Wife*, I was invited to a posh party in Bel Air at the home of publicist

Rupert Allan, a charming man who was publicist for such past luminaries as Grace Kelly, Rock Hudson, Elizabeth Taylor, and many others. This was a glimpse into old Hollywood which had sadly already passed. I had known Rupert's brother, Christopher Allan, also a publicist in New York City who had seen me in the title role of *Anna K*, an adaptation of Tolstoy's *Anna Karenina*. He was ecstatic about my acting and had planned to help me launch my New York acting career in the theatre. Unfortunately, shortly after we met, Chris, who sometimes drank too much, accidently fell out of his high-rise apartment window on the upper East Side in Manhattan. Chris was liked by all who knew him and his memorial at a small church on the East Side was truly memorable. One of his clients, Leontine Price (*Aida* at the Metropolitan Opera) sang acapella, *The Lord's Prayer*. It was pure, simple, and unforgettable.

When I arrived at the Bel Air Party, Rupert greeted me, introducing me to the others as "A wonderful writer from Texas, Katherine Ann Porter." I hastily told him that Porter was another Texas writer — not me. He then introduced me to Jane Wyatt who had played the wife to Robert Young on the television series *Father Knows Best*. Now this was a show I had grown up with as a child. Without a father, I had adopted this show as my surrogate happy family. A television series can be counted on to be there each and every week — where Mothers are kind and loving and Fathers never leave. Yet here's the weird part. When I was introduced to Jane Wyatt, my first response was one of surprise and disappointment that she didn't know who I was! Wasn't she my mother? Such is the power of television!

Several weeks later Rupert invited me to an intimate Oscar Dinner Party and sat me next to Luise Rainer, a two-time Oscar winner for Best Actress (*The Good Earth* and *The Great Ziegfeld)*. Rainer had married well, lived for years in Europe, and now, a widow, had returned to work again in Hollywood. During dinner, Miss Rainer leaned over and told me how much she had enjoyed *The Christmas Wife* and sweetly asked if I might write something for her. I was stunned as she was a famous Oscar-winning actor. Also reminded of the transience of fame.

I must admit to an aversion and handicap in my professional life, and that is, a severe distaste for self-promotion. It is a small miracle to me how fortunate I have been to work in New York and Hollywood, in spite of this aversion.

I had not been working long in Hollywood when I was invited to a friend's house for lunch. Sitting on my right was a Finnish film director — though I did not know it at the time. We spoke of philosophy — which is my passion and turned out to be his as well. He mentioned his years in India with a spiritual teacher. I shared with him something of the years that I had spent in India studying the Advaita Vedanta philosophy with a great Sage. Though I rarely speak of this as it is deeply personal, it seemed natural to do so in this instance. Only at the end of the luncheon did he reveal that he was a film director. Tavi went on to explain that he had come to Hollywood for one purpose: to find a screenwriter who was spiritual.

A few weeks later, during my annual spiritual retreat in India, a young Indian boy on a bicycle rode out to my small, remote village and delivered a telegram from this same Finnish film director/producer, wanting to hire me to adapt the Finnish classic novel, *Wolfbride,* into a screenplay. While meditating thousands of miles away in a remote south Indian village, I got a job. (It was the first time Finland agreed to hire a Writers Guild of America (union) screenwriter and pay accordingly.) *Wolfbride* was the story of a spiritual healer who was burned as a witch in the seventeenth century. I think of it now as my Ingmar Bergman screenplay.

In case you haven't guessed by now, I believe in destiny. One can either work with it or fight it. Having done both, I would recommend tuning in, listening, then following the path of least resistance to that inner calling.

One day my Hollywood agent sent me to Universal Studios to pitch (try and sell) stories to a well-known producer. The story I was prepared to pitch did not interest him, and when asked if I had anything else, off the cuff, I pitched a romantic mother-son comedy/drama loosely based on my recent experience with my son in Texas. Here's the pitch: "A romantic comedy about a mother and son who are roommates in college. It's about a mother who finally grows up and a son who learns how to be young." By the end of the day, *Sammy and Son* became a bidding war between Disney and Universal Studios. Universal won.

My Teacher was coming from India to Austin, Texas for two weeks, so though it was not essential for the script, I asked the Studio for a trip to Austin to research background for *Sammy and Son*, and the studio said yes to a two-week trip, all expenses paid. During my stay there, driving a rental car to the Austin Talks, a car crashed into me, totaling my car. At the moment of impact, I had a vision of the Sage, His Form surrounding me as a protective shield. And though the impact was severe, I was unhurt. Later a friend who was also an astrologer and was attending the Talks, looked at my chart and told the Sage that my chart indicated a possible death at the time of the accident. Whereupon Sri Gurudev said simply, "But she was coming to me."

As to the Universal film project, though I was paid handsomely, our producer, busy producing two popular sitcoms, *Cheers* and *Coach*, had little time to give to *Sammy and Son*.

The film was never made.

Asked to rewrite a teleplay to star Ellen Burstyn, I was flown first class to New York for a week to get to know Burstyn, who was currently starring in a one-woman play on Broadway, a British import called *Shirley Valentine*. She was simply wonderful. It was a pleasant week spending time, sharing meals with Ellen and discovering that she also was very interested in the spiritual. Her teacher was a Sufi master living in France. I returned with a completed script only to learn that the network heads had changed and they now wanted only leading ladies in their twenties, so our project was cancelled. Show Biz!

I was asked by NBC to write a movie for television about the Dalkon Shield Scandal in America. I had never heard of the faulty IUD, but gradually learned of the horrors inflicted on hundreds of women — even when the pharmaceutical company had discovered that the birth control device was flawed. I was teamed with British director David Greene who had won several Emmys — the miniseries *Roots* being one. It was a special treat to work with a seasoned director from the beginning of a project which rarely happens in Hollywood. I interviewed several women victimized by the lethal birth control device then created, from their stories, a composite represented by two characters, their dramatic discovery, followed by the civil action suit brought against the manufacturers. I called it *It's Only Women:*

the Dalkon Shield Scandal. The network was pleased, thinking they would win another Emmy for this important women's issue. They had the previous year won for *Roe versus Wade* about a woman's right to abortion. My only mistake was that I didn't merely write of the scandal but wrote a diatribe against corporate greed and corruption in America. The problem was simply that no corporate sponsor could be found. You don't bite the hand that feeds you.

I still traveled to India each year and spent weekends and summers with Christopher, now at Harvard Law School. I taught graduate screenwriting at USC Film School and wrote screenplays. Now and then, one of my eleven NY plays would be revived which was nice.

A pleasant surprise. I met a fellow Texan composer/songwriter, when he approached me to adapt my *Calamity Jane* play into a musical. I readily gave him permission then was surprised when Alan Jay Freidman insisted that I stay aboard and write the book for the musical. I told him I had never written a musical before and he countered with, "But you know this play better than anyone." This began a delightful collaboration. Jeff Silbar, who had written *Wind Beneath My Wings,* the Bette Midler theme song for the movie, *Beaches,* co-wrote the music with Alan. And Amanda McBroom (known for *The Rose,* another Bette Midler hit song) along with Rand Bishop, country western singer and songwriter, delivered the songs. The musical was first produced with a NY cast in a regional theatre near Atlantic City. Later it was revived a few times. There was Broadway interest which never materialized. I gradually realized that *Calamity Jane* was more an American musical than the current Broadway taste.

With Jeff and Alan at *Calamity Jane* revival, 2014

In 2014, the musical was revived in Orange County and voted the best show of the year. I notified Alan and Jeff to join me to see the show and we agreed to meet at the theatre. I warned Jeff on the phone that I now had white hair, and he replied in kind, "So do I." We all met and the production was a good one plus a pleasant reunion.

When I was writing for the popular CBS television series, *Touched by an Angel,* I created a story, loosely based on my childhood, about a little girl who heard angel voices. The other children taunted her. The younger angel (played by Roma Downey) observing this on the school playground asked, "Human beings are born knowing who they are, why is it they forget?" Then the older angel (played by Della Reese) replies, "They call it education." Once we knew who we are. This forgotten, we spend our lives retracing our steps back home. When this episode aired, I was surprised and disappointed not to see the opening lines which perfectly stated the theme of the one-hour episode. When I asked Martha, our producer, she said, "Oh, we had to cut that so as not to offend teachers!" I suppose it was my line, "They call it education." This also was a moment of realization of how little if any spower a screenwriter has in

Hollywood. In New York, as a playwright, no one could change a single line without my approval.

I was invited by the actor, Ed Asner (*Mary Tyler Moore Show* and others) to sit on a panel in Los Angeles and discuss the theme of censorship. Others on the panel spoke of censorship in communist countries. I surprised myself and others when spontaneously I spoke of being a working screenwriter in Hollywood, and that in America, screenwriters and producers sometimes censor themselves due to commercial pressures. Apart from the episode for *Touched by an Angel* when the producer omitted one of my lines, "They call it education.", one of my best efforts, *It's Only Women: The Dalkon Shield Scandal*, was cancelled on NBC due to pressure from the sponsor, a pharmaceutical corporation. As many writers write to earn their living, they often feel the pressure to censor themselves in order to insure production. After I raised this issue, no one spoke for a while yet afterwards, Ed Asner thanked me for raising this vital point, as it reminded all of us of what is true: self-censorship in a capitalist society.

I began my writing life, writing for myself. Luckily, others responded to the stories, plays, screenplays, and books. And many awards confirmed this for me, encouraging me to continue. It is my experience that when I write with integrity, the work often finds its audience. And, more importantly, I have kept faith with my soul.

The only journey is the one within.

Rainer Marie Rilke

A nice unexpected surprise came when I received an extra residual in the mail. It seems that this *Touched by an Angel* episode was Oprah Winfrey's favorite and she screened a scene on her popular talk show. I suspect she identified with the little girl who heard the angels sing.

It is my feeling that some stories already exist in the ether, and my job is simply to bring them down to the gross level. The best times are when I seem to disappear altogether and the story writes itself. It passes through me, but is not really mine — a kind of visitation, if you will.

I see visions which I could not see
with my ordinary eye.

Maxine Hong Kingston (*Woman Warrior*)

When I wrote the Virginia Woolf play, *On the Edge*, Woolf's diaries and letters had not yet been published so I had to make up the dialogue. A couple of years after the play was written and produced, they were published and several lines in my play were the same as those found in Woolf's letters and diaries! And when I sat down to write the reincarnation Irish screenplay, *Second Chance*, twenty-two years after my waking vision in Ireland at the ruins of a ninth century monastery, every detail I saw was historical fact! The Irish story had to wait until I turned my attention to writing screenplays as it had to be an epic film — not a play or book.

This process of listening to the unconscious is greatly aided by listening and recording your dreams, which inevitably speak the language of the unconscious, and can serve as a guide. William Blake might refer to this as "the crooked way being the right way." It has been my experience that sometimes story ideas may come through dreams at night.

One night I dreamt of an *angel* returned to earth because he was not yet ready for heaven. Denied his wings because he was still too attached to earthly pleasures, he was asked to undergo a trial on earth, to earn his wings. I recorded the dream in my journal then thought no more about it. About ten days later, my agent had a call from megastar Dolly Parton's company. Dolly had been scouting for a good Christmas story for television, and after two years, had not found one she liked. Because of the success of my film, *The Christmas Wife*, they thought I might come up with something. Immediately, I thought of the angel dream. I switched genders from male to female angel, and while driving to the meeting, developed the story, set it two weeks before Christmas, and called it, *Unlikely Angel*.

Now, please understand that I do not read magazines or Variety, or other books which gossip about what stars like. I was simply guided by my intuition — a faculty I have come to trust far more than the rational brain. So, I was not aware that Dolly Parton is simply mad about angels. I walked into her Hollywood home and saw angel sculptures in the garden, a tapestry of angels on the wall, and little angel ornaments placed here and there on several tables. Eureka! I was home free. This story would sell. And, it did, to Disney Studios for the one and only Dolly Parton (and Roddy McDowell). *Unlikely Angel* had the highest ratings when it aired on CBS — beaten only by the NFL football game. Never underestimate the popularity of football!

In my experience, there is no neat formula for creative success. The little bugger keeps changing on you. Yes, craft matters but it can never, ever replace the Source of creativity which lies deep within the psyche of each individual, waiting to be tapped. As in dreams, creativity arises from the unconscious. Our job is to create an empty space in our conscious minds for the unconscious to emerge with its bountiful gifts. We have only to allow the process to flow. And above all, try not to separate creative work from life as George Balanchine had taught me years before. The general neurosis of our time is that we are split, lacking what is essential: a spiritual or soul connection. To live or write only from the logical brain — one part of yourself —

results in a fragmented story as well as a fragmented life. Somehow *Buddha and the Dancing Girl* have to merge.

In the best art, form is the outcome of feeling, not thinking. Thinking — though a valuable tool — is only handmaiden to a much deeper process.

> It is the inexplicable presence of the thing not
>> named
> the emotional aura that gives high quality to the
> novel or to drama, as well as to poetry itself.
>
> Willa Cather

I usually write mornings and sometimes review the day's work in the afternoon. It is my practice to push through, not stopping, until I have a first draft. However, while writing *Unlikely Angel,* I hit a road block: the perennial Act II problem in screenwriting. I knew what had to happen in the plot. I just didn't quite know 'how' it would happen. After an hour of forcing or 'pushing the river', I sensibly decided to let it go for a while. As is my custom, I left the house, drove to the athletic club near my home, and swam laps in our near Olympic size lap pool, totally letting go of the story and the block. Then, the miracle occurred. At the thirteenth lap, the solution came! I had consciously let go of the problem, allowing the space for the unconscious to take over and solve it. There are indeed invisible helpers at work when you least expect them!

> When the tank runs dry,
> You have only to leave it alone
> And it will fill up again.
>
> Mark Twain

Though I am grateful for my seven years writing for Hollywood as work was plentiful and my son was doing well at Harvard, I found living in Los Angeles isolating. I look back at those four years living there as time spent as a writing machine and little else. Outside my window in the downstairs Hollywood apartment, was a parking lot with one small tree and a few leaves. Very Samuel Beckett. That was the only view I had from my desk for those four years in the City of the Angels. Besides, after living in Manhattan for twenty years, somehow LA did not feel like a real city. In NY, I would daily rub elbows with humanity every day on the street. Here's one example of what I mean. After moving to California, I was invited back to NY to teach, and was on a city bus. An older woman got on and could not speak English. The driver asked her what language, and she replied, "Ruskie". Then he casually turned back to the other passengers and shouted, "Anyone here speak Russian?" Sure enough, from the rear of the bus, a man came forward and translated for them. That's NY.

Living in Los Angeles, a car culture. I would sometimes go two days or more without speaking with anyone in person. I knew it was time to leave, but stalled. Work was good, and my son was doing well in school. Yet another nudge was needed to get me out of LA — as it had before to leave NY. It soon came in a most unexpected manner.

The Los Angeles Riots of 1992, major outbreak of violence, looting, and arson in Los Angeles that began on April 29, 1992, in response to the acquittal of four white Los Angeles policemen connected with the severe beating of an African American motorist in March 1991. 1992 was the highest crime rate ever seen in Los Angeles. I was living alone in Hollywood near the worst of the riots and outside my front door, heard gunshots on my street. Stores a few blocks away were burning, looting, and deafening sirens heard everywhere. This was the nudge. I would soon leave. But where would I go?

> My barn having burned down,
> I can now see the moon.
>
> Mizuta Masahide (17th century Japanese poet)

Part VI Ojai, 1993-current

The privilege of a lifetime is to become who you truly are.

C. G. Jung

Catherine, hiking in Ojai, CA, 1994

Coming home is the longest journey and the most important. I travel the world and seldom rest from teaching workshops both here and abroad. After years of wandering, I stop, become quite still, and turn within … only to realize that home has been there all along, for home is the centered Self. Once you are at home within, you are at home anywhere and everywhere. There is nowhere to go, no one to be. And yet, I am very fortunate to have found both my tribe and my natural home in Ojai, California.

During my first stay in India in 1968, I had met Mark Lee, then a high school teacher at the Krishnamurti Rishi Valley School near Bangalore. I spent a month there and wrote a play about a sad love story whose soul mate was waiting to be born again and could only contact his love on the subtle plane, *The Hill*, which I directed for the students. Years later when I moved from Manhattan to Hollywood, a friend of mine suggested I get in touch with Mark, then the President of the Krishnamurti Foundation for America and founder of the Oak Grove School in Ojai — not far from Los Angeles. Our mutual friend was actor Roshan Seth, best known for playing India's first Prime Minister, Nehru, in the Oscar-winning film, *Gandhi*, directed by Richard Attenborough. I did get in touch with Mark who invited me to stay with him and his wife, Asha, in Ojai, and participate on two panels during the annual Krishnamurti Gathering. Now new friends came to welcome me to where K had lived and died only a few years before, creating a cyclic return, so many years after I had met J. Krishnamurti in Bombay.

On the first time driving to Ojai, an unexpected thing happened. When I saw the exit sign for Ojai, I had an intuition that one day I would live there. Now I knew nothing of Ojai before that first visit yet the energy of this mountain valley was such that I felt completely at home. It is no accident that the 1937 film classic, *Lost Horizons* about Shangri La, an idyllic, hidden valley, was shot in Ojai. Three years later I did move there from Hollywood and have lived here happily for the last twenty-six years.

I had quit teaching at USC (University of Southern California Film School) and began to be invited to lead writing workshops at the Esalen and Omega Institutes and many other venues both in the States and abroad, as well as various writers conferences and film festivals. Locally, I became one of the three final judges in The Ojai International Film Festival for the next twenty years. I respected the theme of this festival, 'Enriching the human spirit through film.' In Hollywood, I would write only consciousness-raising films — no gratuitous sex or violence — so this festival theme merited my support. And, it felt right to do some community service where I had chosen to make my home.

Though I still travel extensively, Ojai remains a tranquil

harbor and a good place to write as well. Here an introspective life, teaching globally (UK, Greece, Singapore, India, Kuwait, Italy, NY, etc.), writing books, plays, films, and online courses, leading various workshops, working as a writing consultant, trips to family and to my spiritual home in India, so life is seldom dull.

My now departed friend, the artist and author Anne Truitt, once told me over a dinner at Yaddo, "You know, Catherine, life is really very long." We went on to discuss how we lead many lives, even in this one life. She was right. Though she is sorely missed, her fine paintings and sculptures remain in the Metropolitan Art Museum and other galleries.

I began my working life as an actor in New York then playwright, later Hollywood screenwriter and more recently, an author of books, with a parallel career teaching writing and self-healing with writing now for over thirty years. Throw in a twenty-year marriage and raising a son, and it's been quite a journey. After two decades teaching graduate school in New York, University of Texas, and later USC in Los Angeles), I opted to hit the road leading *The Way of Story* and *Heal Your Self with Writing* workshops. The workshop life began at the Esalen Institute in Big Sur, a teaching environment that did not hamper me with academic restraints but allowed me to pioneer new experiential approaches to writing all forms of narrative and dramatic writing. It was also in this generative setting that I developed my ideas on how creativity can become a powerful tool for self-healing and inner discovery.

Now, I teach globally, and human nature is amazingly the same yet, at the same time, totally diverse. I am never bored with teaching as each one's story is unique, and I am grateful to my many students and consultant clients over the decades who allow me to learn while teaching them.

Heal Your Self with Writing in Kuwait

After teaching in India, Singapore, Greece, England, Spain, and Mexico as well as all over the U.S., I was invited to teach in Kuwait which borders Iraq. When they called to invite me, I assumed they wanted *The Way of Story* writing workshop, but they said, "Oh, no, we want the healing one." I harbored some concern as my contract included a promise not to offend the Muslim faith, and to agree not to discuss reincarnation or angels. I asked if there was a dress code, imagining myself teaching in a birka! The response was 'no' except no mini-skirts or sleeveless blouses. No alcohol — not a problem — though, while travelling business class in the air, I did enjoy a glass of red wine with my meals, preparing for what would be a new adventure.

After twenty hours in the air and eight hours in airports, I arrived a zombie. I had done some homework to counter my ignorance of their history.

Kuwait with four million population, is wedged between Iraq to the north and Saudi Arabia to the south. The Arabian name "Kuwait" means fortress. After the first World War, Kuwait emerged as an independent sheikdom under the protection of the British Empire until they gained their independence in 1961. In 1990, Kuwait was invaded and annexed by neighboring Iraq. The seven month-long Iraqi occupation came to an end after direct military intervention by the United States. Over seven-hundred and seventy Kuwaiti oil wells were set ablaze by the Iraqi army, resulting in a major environmental and economic catastrophe. Twelve years later, Kuwait saw another massive foreign military presence as it served as a springboard for the U.S.-led campaign in 2003 to oust Iraqi leader Saddam Hussein. Kuwait is at present a constitutional monarchy with a parliamentary system of government. Described as the most liberal country in the region, Kuwait is the eighth richest country in the world per capita with the fifth largest oil reserves.

As I entered Kuwait City, recently rebuilt, it seemed more like a Hollywood set for a futuristic sci-fi movie. Stunning, pristine clean, and no lack of Lexus or Jaguars rushing here and there. The *Heal Your Self with Writing* seminar lasted only three days for ten women and one man. All but two of the women wore full birka with only their faces visible. Most were professional women, with Ph.D.s., M.D.s, etc. and had attended private schools abroad and spoke English well. My first words when I greeted the class was, "We are all children of Abraham." The response was enthusiastic and moving. The workshop went well with a deep response from all. "It was an inspirational life changing workshop" said one birka-clad woman.

Bill Moyers, a fellow Texan, once commented that he understood what community was when in East Africa, he had sat around a campfire with natives sharing their life stories. I felt the same with these strong women and one sensitive man who allowed feeling through old wounds and collective censorship to blossom into transformative healing and tolerance. To end with one man's own words: "Love is the word that explains the feeling I have towards you and your course. You have released bottled up emotions within me, and you, your book, and course are a treasure that I will forever hold on to. Thank you!" Responses such as these make it worthwhile in spite of the jetlag!

In 1993, on my annual trip to Kerala in south India, I had suffered a severe heat stroke. It had been the hottest summer in over fifty years, reaching 140 degrees Fahrenheit with high humidity — over two hundred Indians had died that summer. For three years, I could not write or exercise. Finally, it was discovered that my thyroid had ceased to function. Given little thyroid pills, I came back to life. Still, it was an impasse, a turning point, and I wasn't sure what to do next.

One night, back home in Ojai, a dream came to guide me when I most needed it. The dream was simple: A woman was six months pregnant and would deliver a new child three months from now. I knew to be open for clues as to the practical meaning of the dream, mainly that in three months, a new life would begin. A fellow writer whom I had not yet met called, inviting me to lunch. During the meal, she mentioned she was a student at Pacifica Graduate Institute in Santa Barbara. When I heard the name, I intuitively knew that this was my next step. The next morning, I drove to Santa Barbara, only forty minutes from Ojai, and asked to submit an admission form. Told the deadline was the next day and that the semester would begin in three months, I smiled. *Three months*. Then I said, "That's all right, a dream guided me to do this." Pacifica is a graduate school of Depth Psychology, mainly studying C. G. Jung. I chose to focus on 'Depth Psychology and Archetypal Mythology'. When I told my pragmatic Texas mother, surprised, she said, "What are you going to do with a graduate degree in Mythology?" I replied, "It's not what I'm going to do with Mythology but what Mythology is going to do with me." (I understood only later what this meant.) So, after teaching graduate school in NY,

Austin, and LA for several years, I became for the first time, a graduate student.

I continued to write for Hollywood (*Touched by an Angel* series) and do rewrites on film scripts (*Poe: The Dark Angel* and *Sargent Presley*) and teach here and there while going full time to Pacifica. Though a challenge, it was possible to work and go to school as classes met one weekend a month (12 hours a day) and one month in the summer.

Pacifica proved to be a wonderfully timely, healing journey. Also, we had to write a multitude of papers which helped me to discover my voice in prose, as I usually wrote dramatic writing and dialogue in plays and screenplays. After two years, I earned a Master's Degree then experienced what I at first took to be a writer's block.

Friends in Santa Fe had invited me to visit. A few minutes from downtown Santa Fe, Danny and Merrie have a lovely home with a large courtyard and welcoming hammocks. Weak and listless, I spent hours lying in a hammock watching New Mexico's amazing panorama of clouds. One afternoon, half asleep, I had a waking vision and heard these words, "The Way of Story". Soon I realized that my so-called writers block was that I had always before written plays or movies and that I was to now write books. I had to let go of what I was and open to what is now. The first book was called *The Way of Story: the craft and soul of writing.* Then came *Heal Your Self with Writing* that was given a Nautilus Book Award. And then *What Story Are You Living?* I also wrote a collection of stories for children of all ages called *True Fables: Stories from Childhood.*

I had rented an apartment in downtown Ojai for three years before I bought a home. Dennis, the realtor, drove me to a corner house about a five-minute drive from downtown Ojai. Before getting out of the car, near the door, I spotted a large hibiscus plant with bright red flowers and knew that 'this was the house'. Outside the house that I had built in India was an identical hibiscus plant with red flowers. I turned to Dennis and said, "This is the one." He blinked and said, "But you haven't seen inside yet." It was the one and the sale went through quickly.

After I moved into the three-year old house in Ojai, CA, I engaged a Buddhist monk from Sri Lanka, visiting Los Angeles, to do a ritual cleansing and blessing of my new home. The monk arrived with all his Tibetan bowls, bells, incense, and sacred texts. The ceremony rituals would last three hours. At first, he walked outside circling the house, then inside, and surprised me by what he said. He quietly viewed my many sacred paintings and Tibetan tangkas then pronounced, "All the art depicts the Light yet there is nothing to symbolize the dark side." Of course, it had never occurred to me before, but something within knew he was right. For balance, one must include both the Light and Dark, else the dark might involuntarily enter my home. I found in my garden a cement gargoyle and at the monk's bidding, placed it behind the front door in the corner. I pondered that this was why in medieval times, apart from guarding the churches, they created so many gargoyles outside the great cathedrals, especially near the entrance to a sacred space. Then at the housewarming a few days later, a couple I knew from Los Angeles came with an unusual gift. It was a demon mask from Borneo made of small sea shells. "Perfect", I exclaimed, as I opened the gift, and proceeded to share with them the story of the monk's response to my home full of Light in the art and no symbol of the Dark.

Two former suitors from my New York days came to Ojai with proposals of marriage. Though not tempted, I have maintained friendships with both men who happily later found wives and children. I have lived contentedly with Missy Prissy the cat for the last eighteen years. Cats are so much easier than husbands or children — and you don't have to send them to Harvard either!

I surprised myself when between writing books, one day I sat down and wrote *Freud's Oracle,* my 11th play, based on the true story of H.D. (Hilda Doolittle), the American poet who had a two-year analysis with Sigmund Freud in Vienna in the 1930s

255

and persuaded him to leave Nazi Austria with his family and move to London where she was living.

Though I had not acted for many years, I decided to stage the one-woman play in Ojai and perform the role myself. My intention was to only do the show once before publishing it. Yet each time I would do it, someone in the audience would invite me to do it elsewhere: Santa Fe, New Orleans, Santa Barbara, Dallas, and three times in Ojai at other venues, until I had performed it in seven productions. It was nice to know that acting is like riding a bicycle in that you don't forget how. However, I knew that I had little interest in returning to acting, preferring to write instead — and teach. Besides, I wanted to spend more time in Ojai, my Shangri La.

Since the early 1970s, I have also served as a psychic reader for many decades. Psychic since the age of seven, I was asked to become a reader and told that this could help others. It came about like this. I was living in New York City and working as an actor when Bebita, an older friend from Argentina, called to say she was coming to New York expressly to see me. She told me that her former nanny, a Romany gypsy from Spain, had taught her a very unique system of reading ordinary playing cards as fortune telling. The gypsy told my friend that she must promise to teach one person this unique system of reading fortunes before she died. My friend then told me she believed I was the one to continue the legacy. The following three weeks, she taught me the intricate system. Then after bestowing on me this unique gift, she passed away three days later. Fortunately, her daughter had come from Paris to be with her mother at the end.

Bebita had also met Sri Gurudev in India and attended the Paris Talks. I sat beside her bed when she passed and stayed on to meditate. Next to her bed was a small vase with incense from India. Opening my eyes, though there was no wind or air conditioning in the room, the lit incense stick moved pointing to just beyond where I sat. I turned around and saw a photograph of our Teacher on the piano which I had not before seen. His Presence permeated the entire room. Bebita had wished to be cremated and her ashes tossed into the ocean near Manhattan. So her daughter and I carried a package of her ashes onto the Staten Island Ferry. Knowing it was illegal to pour ashes into the water there, we devised a strategy. Her daughter would stand guard as I poured the ashes off the side of the rear deck. All went well and Bebita's wish was satisfied.

Gypsy Fortune Telling

At first, for years, I did card readings only for friends gratuitously. Then an internationally known medium from Bali, whom I would sometimes read for, advised me to begin to read cards professionally. At first, I hesitated but then within the same week, another psychic friend and professional reader, told me the same thing, and as I regard both highly, I felt it was time to serve Spirit in this way. My clients are now from all over the world and the readings come through the same on the phone as in person. And, happily, I can do this work from home in tranquil Ojai where I try to remain as much as possible.

Yet even in this Ojai oasis, sorrow comes. Within one year, many close friends passed away, eight in all. Soon I was afraid to answer the phone wondering if it signaled another death.

My small world threatens to be underpopulated.

Alec Guinness, *My Name Escapes Me*

The price of staying on, as we get older, is that people we love fall away. Friends. Parents. Pets.

Mother and I had become closer in her last thirty years, and I am grateful for that. Afterall, you only have one mother. She finally gave up trying to change me, continued to grow, and became more tolerant. And I became more patient and tolerant of those with different values. After an intervention I staged to expose her alcoholism, a woman of strong will, Mother stopped drinking, living on for two more decades. Initially opposed to

Mother and Catherine in Ojai

my marriage to a non-Christian foreigner, she later became a hostess to foreign students at a nearby university. I spent more time with her in Dallas, Ojai, and Hawaii, especially during the last three years when refusing to move to Ojai, she had to leave her home and enter assisted care. We had a celebration of her 90th birthday with over fifty friends and relatives which she thoroughly enjoyed. It is so important to celebrate the lives of loved ones while they're still here. I visited more and more often, and fortunately, was with her the final ten days. She passed away in her sleep three months before her 91st birthday.

In my recent play, *Freud's Oracle*, there's a line I made up that H. D. says about her own mother's death, "There comes a time for all of us when you suddenly realize you are no longer anyone's child. However, as we well know, death need not end a deep relationship." Now six years after her passing, I can definitely state that death does not end a deep relationship.

Here's a recent example of synchronicity (apparent coincidence yet connected in some way). Three months ago, I had lunch with a friend who was talking about a boy she loved in high school who had died in his twenties. She commented on how she still feels him close to her though he's been dead for many years. I shared that I felt the same about my mother who is still around though she passed away six years ago. Five minutes later in my car, I turned on the radio. It was the classical radio station, and this was the first thing I heard: "Now we have a birthday request from Cathy Jones (not me) from Southern California whose birthday is tomorrow (same as mine). The request is Debussy's *Clair de Lune*." This was my mother's favorite piece and for her memorial, I had arranged for a pianist to play it just before the Memorial Service began. Yes, Mother, I know you're here!

To truly honor those loved ones who have passed on, we must integrate the legacy left to us and give something back to those still living. Life is resilient, demanding from us to live fully to our best potential, and then to pass on what we have been given. Nothing is ever truly lost, only recycled.

While in Sills Maria, Switzerland walking by the lake, the philosopher Nietzsche who had challenged religion in the mid-19th century, had an epiphany. He realized that despite human suffering, man must embrace the whole of life, returning again and again to all experience, including pain and suffering and this presents an eternal return and life affirmation.

> One must never despair if something is lost — a person
> or a happiness;
> Everything comes back more gloriously.
> What falls away, falls away;
> What belongs to us remains with us,
> For everything proceeds according to laws greater than
> our insight.
> One must live in oneself and think of the whole in life,
> Of all its millions of possibilities, expanses, and futures,
> In the face of which there is nothing past or lost.
>
> Rainer Maria Rilke

Losing so many loved ones — including Sasha, Missy's brother as well as Missy herself three years later — both great feline companions who are buried together in front of a stone Buddha in my back garden. So many losses inspired me to write my sixth online course, *Shifting Perspective on Death*. As of today, the six online courses have over 56,000 subscribers. I see it as another form of teaching in today's modern world. And the writing remains, for me, the greatest therapy.

Paris Talks with Sri Gurudev, 1978

Corinne, a French disciple, had been struggling with the final stage of cancer. Though her doctors had given her only three months to live, it was now seven months. She was waiting to see the Sage one last time when He came to Paris. After a daily talk downstairs, a few of us were upstairs standing near His chair. One outspoken and rather dramatic French disciple, Jane said, "I hate life. I hate everything about life."

After a pause, Corinne's gentle voice was heard. "Gurudev, I have the opposite problem. I love life. I love everything about life." The Sage gazed at her for a moment then asked, "You say you love life. That you love everything about life?" "Yes", she quickly agreed. Then the Sage in a most tender voice said, "Well then you must love Death. For Death, too, is a part of life."

The entire atmosphere in the room changed. We all knew that Corinne was soon to die, and that she had through sheer will, stayed on to see the Sage one last time. Silence reigned as He continued to look at her, and it was as if she grasped his gaze and hung on with what strength she could muster. Though her eyes filled with tears, her face was radiant. Bliss had trumped death. Death *is* but another part of life.

A few years later, on my annual visit to India, I was invited to teach screenwriting in Singapore for two weeks, after which I flew to south India to visit the Sage. I had only ten days due to work obligations in Hollywood. Arriving late afternoon, I learned that a dear friend and fellow disciple, Emile, was ill in hospital. It was suggested that I wait until the next morning to visit him, but something told me not to wait. So, I took an auto rickshaw, arriving early evening at the hospital. Emile, an Egyptian disciple, had lived for years in Kerala in order to be near our Teacher, and we had been friends for many years. After a few words, I simply sat in silence next to his bed, and turned within, focusing on the Sage. After a moment, Sri Gurudev's presence filled the room. He was there. Then Emile, barely conscious, sat up and called His name out loudly, "Gurudev! Gurudev!". Emile's face was radiant as he lay back, eyes now closed, smiling and completely at rest. I quietly took my leave and when arriving back at my house, was told that Emile had passed away soon after I had left the hospital.

Some years later, the unimaginable happened. At this time, I was at the Esalen Institute in Big Sur, California, where I teach each year. Yet this time, I had been invited to come as an assistant to Dr. Peter Levine who taught somatic psychology to treat trauma.

While I was there, Christopher called to say that our Teacher was dying. We both decided to fly to India. Knowing I had first to drive home to Ojai from Big Sur to get my passport and pack, I planned to leave the next morning. However, early the following day, Christopher called again to say "Mother, He is gone." Sri Gurudev left the body, Feb 2001.

Considering whether to now go to India, I sat alone on the edge of a cliff overlooking the Pacifica Ocean in Big Sur and meditated. The answer came from within. Experiencing that it is all One and nowhere to go, I called my son to say that I had decided not to fly to India, and he replied that he was going anyway.

I told Dr. Levine that I would be unable to assist in his class and simply withdrew to have a personal retreat. Sitting quietly outside near the Dining Room overlooking the Pacific Ocean, a young woman I did not know approached and asked if I would like to join in a Sweat Lodge soon to begin. In India, death is considered impure so when someone dies close to you, those connected are deemed impure for a certain length of time and sometimes, certain rituals are done. The Native American Sweat Lodge is a ritual of purification. I accepted and was walking to the Tepee Sweat Lodge when an attractive young man in his twenties walked toward me singing "Ram, Ram, Sita

Ram," the hymn to the epic Indian Sage, Sri Rama. Then sitting in the sweat lodge with about seven others, we were each asked to say our names. A woman directly across from where I sat, looked straight at me and said, "My name is Moksha." Moksha in Sanskrit means liberation. The Presence of my Guru was felt so strongly that I knew beyond doubt that neither Death nor geography could affect the Presence of Truth and the Sage.

Not long afterwards my son and I returned to India together. Like many other disciples, I expected to be sad, but, to my surprise, the atmosphere was entirely the opposite. It resembled more a wedding celebration. Try as I might, sadness simply would not stick. The Presence of the Sage was so strong that in spite of ourselves, we were lifted up, even joyous and carried to the Light.

I remembered, too, forty years earlier, asking the Sage, "What happens with the relationship when the Guru leaves the body?" and His response, "The relationship with the Guru will be even stronger." It is so as He is within. His words to me then, as to so many others, were seeds planted firmly in the heart to later bloom and be more fully understood. The gift that keeps on giving. Such is the living legacy of a true Sage.

> You pay a price for what you do,
> And you pay a price for what you don't do.
>
> Louise Nevelson, sculptor

No life is perfect. One does pay a price one way or another. That is the deal. No doubt I could have done much more in my acting and writing career if I had been more ambitious, more savvy, better at business and self-promotion, and sometimes I regret that. That I had not served the work better. Yet it would not have been true to who I am, and I believe that it matters to be the best 'true you' one can be. We have a duty to our deeper Self to be true to who and what we truly are. How? By being still, turning within, and listening to that deeper Self.

Granted, flying to India after each small success and being weeks or months there, is not the smartest career move. Yet my time in India mattered more. In the end, there is always choice — price or no price. Like most Americans, I am a doer. Over five decades of meditation has not tempered my desire to act, express, reach out, and to move. I shall probably never retire from writing and teaching so the dance continues. The plain fact is I like to work creatively and feel more myself when I am writing or teaching. There is a certain joy in giving back what you have learned and hearing from students that 'this workshop changed their life'. I have recently written several stories for children in *True Fables*. Perhaps having had a son and now two grandchildren has inspired this.

As for the 'still private' ashram in India, none knew what would come next after His passing. I continued to go to India to visit the family. However, though the presence of where a Sage has lived and left the body remains powerful, I could not understand the new directions the ashram was going. What I admired about Sri Gurudev was the integrity of His teaching which never swayed to the religious or cult-like gatherings so prevalent in modern times today. His — as His Father's before — was a pure, direct approach to the Truth. On my last visit, it had become less and less a joyous atmosphere but instead one of fear and suspicion — a kind of reformation had begun. I told myself that I must not judge. Perhaps this reformation was needed in the interim. How could I know what the Sage intended? Only a Sage can truly understand a Sage. I received a request from the director of one of my plays to come back for casting before rehearsals began. Here was a legitimate reason to leave yet I could not get a booking on the airline as it was high season. After trying three times to get a seat, I accepted defeat and resolved that I would remain for the next ten days as originally planned.

That afternoon, however, a very strange occurrence happened. I was in front of my house in Kerala and walking toward a low wall which surrounds our property there. In front of the wall was a pile of dry leaves when suddenly a four-foot long poisonous snake bolted out from the leaves, its head and upper body raised a foot in the air as it slithered hurriedly and directly toward me as if to attack its prey. I yelled and ran up the stairs into the house. This was no ordinary occurrence as there seemed to be something diabolic in its energy, as if it was a warning for me to get out. I told myself I would try one last time to book a flight home. I called the airline and was told that only a few minutes before, someone had cancelled so there was one seat available. I took it. This meant I had to pack and leave within the hour as it was a three-and-a-half-hour drive to the airport from our village. I went to my Teacher's house to take leave of the family then returned to book a taxi and pack as hurriedly as possible. To this day, there is no doubt in my mind that Spirit had sent a messenger forcing me to leave, for my own well-being.

Sometimes after a great Sage or Being such as Christ or the Buddha leaves, in their wake, ambitions arise and religions and institutions come into play, often diffusing the higher energy of those great beings who inspired them. Then I recalled a story Gurudev had shared with me about His father. Years before, my Teacher's father and Guru was visited by the head of the Rockefeller Institute who was deeply impressed with the Sage. He told him that he would allot any amount of money needed and would make of him an institution. The Guru smiled, politely refusing his offer, and simply replied, "Sir, I am already an institution."

Later on, studying Jungian psychology at Pacifica Graduate Institute had created a balance with my decades of Advaita Vedanta. C.G. Jung helped me preserve my humanity and individualize my spiritual understanding, allowing it to become a more authentic fit.

My old friend, Joe Campbell, once wrote about the Arthurian legends in *Pathways to Bliss,* a posthumously published book: From the Arthurian romance, *La Queste del Saint Graal*, by an anonymous 13th c. monk, the knights were assembled around the round table, planning to go in search of the Holy Grail. They thought it would be a disgrace to go forth in a group. Each entered the Forest Adventurous at that point which he himself had chosen, where it was darkest, where there is no path. When there's a way or path, it is someone else's path; each human being is a unique phenomenon. The idea is to find our own pathway to bliss. In Buddhism, the third station along the path to fulfillment is *apotheosis*, where you realize that you are what you are seeking. The ultimate example of this is when Gautama Shakyamuni achieves Buddhahood and realizes, "I am the Buddha." Those early imprints of Japan persist, when I saw Buddha and the dancing girl, which later became an archetypal metaphor for my life to come: a longing for the spiritual combined with the compulsion to express creatively. The difference now is that I need no longer swing back and forth.

Thanks to having met the Householder Sage, India is firmly rooted in the geography of my heart. The pendulum now still, as the tension of opposites has finally merged.

I continue to write and to accept invitations to travel the world leading workshops, yet always returning to Ojai, a small town without small town people, where the atmosphere guides one simply 'to be'. And, as time permits, periodically to sit down and write another story, book, play, or film — while teaching others to do the same — either in person or through online courses.

All in all, though not perfect, it has been a good life, a learning life, a creative life, and for that, I am grateful. The spiritual transformation has made it possible for me, wherever I am, to center then act. To respond rather than react. To flow rather than simply move for movement's sake. Ambition becomes dharma.

Enlightenment occurs through the persistent striving of an earnest seeker and the Grace of a true Teacher. Realization is not a destination as once thought, but rather a moment to moment living of that awakened Truth. As waves and sea are nothing but water so *Buddha & the Dancing Girl* are but One. One. One.

Epilogue

> It is returning, at last it is coming home to me — my
> own Self and those parts of it that have long been
> abroad and scattered among all things and accidents.
>
> Nietzsche, *Thus Spoke Zarathustra*

Looking back over these many years has provided insights and gratitude for what became an unconventional yet creative adventure. Though writing is a solitary act, one does not travel alone as there are helpers along the way. Some are mentioned in the book, others, though remembered, are not.

Special thanks to my first readers on past books as well as this one. To Dr. Betty Sue Flowers for her sharp editorial skills and longtime friendship, and to Dr. Dianne Skafte for her perceptive comments and continual support. As the song says, "I get by with a little help from my friends."

As said in Sri Nisargadatta's book, *I Am That*:

Life and work become an offering to the Absolute, this
    the soul's journey towards wholeness.
In the immensity of Consciousness, a light appears — a
    tiny point
that moves rapidly and traces shapes, thoughts and
    feelings,
like a pen writing on paper. And the ink which leaves a
    trace is memory.
You are that tiny point and by your movement the
    world is ever recreated.

Also by Catherine Ann Jones

TELEVISION

Child of Destiny (Last Queen of Hawaii)

It's Only Women (The Dalkon Shield Scandal)

Death of an Innocent Child (starring Ellen Burstyn)

Summertime (Hallmark)

Touched by an Angel (series)

FILM & CABLE

The Pact

Sammy and Son (Universal feature)

Wolfbride

Poe: The Dark Angel

The Christmas Wife (starring Jason Robards, Julie Harris) — HBO, 4 Emmy Nominations

Unlikely Angel (starring Dolly Parton) — CBS

Angel Passing (co-writer), (starring Hume Cronyn, Calista Flockhart) —15 Awards

PLAYS

Freud's Oracle

Calamity Jane

Calamity Jane the Musical (Best Production 2015)

The Women of Cedar Creek (NY Drama League Award, Beverly Hills Theatre Guild Award)

The Myth of Annie Beckman

On the Edge: The Final Years of Virginia Woolf (NEA Award)

Somewhere-in-Between

Difficult Friends

The Hill

The Friend

A Fairytale for Adults

BOOKS: PRINT, KINDLE, & AUDIBLE

The Way of Story: The Craft & Soul of Writing

Heal Your Self with Writing (Nautilus Book Award)

What Story Are You Living?

Freud's Oracle

True Fables: Stories from Childhood

Buddha & the Dancing Girl: A Creative Life

About the Author

Catherine Ann Jones holds a graduate degree in Depth Psychology and Archetypal Mythology from Pacifica Graduate Institute where she has also taught. After playing major roles in over fifty plays on and off-Broadway, she became disappointed by the lack of good roles for women and wrote a play, *On the Edge*, about Virginia Woolf and her struggle with madness in a world gone mad, Hitler and WWII. The play won a National Endowment for the Arts Award. Several of her eleven plays have won multiple awards, including *Calamity Jane* (both play and musical), *The Women of Cedar Creek,* and *Freud's Oracle,* and are produced both in and out of New York. Her films include *The Christmas Wife* (Jason Robards & Julie Harris) — four Emmy nominations, *Unlikely Angel* (Dolly Parton), and the popular TV series, *Touched by an Angel.* A Fulbright Research Scholar to India studying shamanism, she has taught at The New School University, University of Southern California, and the Esalen and the Omega Institutes. Her books, *The Way of Story: the craft & soul of writing, Heal Your Self with Writing* (Nautilus Book Award 2014), *What Story Are You Living, Freud's Oracle, True Fables: Stories from Childhood,* and *Buddha and the Dancing Girl* are used in many schools, including New York University writing programs. Her latest book, *East is West (Stories of India),* will be published in 2022. Based in Ojai, California, she leads *The Way of Story* and *Heal Your Self with Writing* workshops throughout the United States, Europe, Middle East, and Asia. Over 56,000 have subscribed to her six online courses. For plays, blog, interviews, workshop schedule, keynote talks, psychic readings, online courses, and writing consultant services, please visit:

www.wayofstory.com

www.ingramcontent.com/pod-product-compliance
Lightning Source LLC
Chambersburg PA
CBHW061517020726
47502CB00006B/2120